Cooking for a Beautiful Woman

Larry Levine

Cooking for a Beautiful Woman

The Tastes and Tales of a Wonderful Life

*A Memoir
with Recipes for the Home Cook*

www.tabletalkatlarrys.com

Copyright © 2019 Larry Levine.
A project of Larry Levine & Associates

All rights reserved. No part of this book may be used or reproduced by any means, graphic, electronic, or mechanical, including photocopying, recording, taping or by any information storage retrieval system without the written permission of the author except in the case of brief quotations embodied in critical articles and reviews.

Archway Publishing books may be ordered through booksellers or by contacting:

Archway Publishing
1663 Liberty Drive
Bloomington, IN 47403
www.archwaypublishing.com
1 (888) 242-5904

Because of the dynamic nature of the Internet, any web addresses or links contained in this book may have changed since publication and may no longer be valid. The views expressed in this work are solely those of the author and do not necessarily reflect the views of the publisher, and the publisher hereby disclaims any responsibility for them.

Any people depicted in stock imagery provided by Getty Images are models, and such images are being used for illustrative purposes only. Certain stock imagery © Getty Images.

ISBN: 978-1-4808-6460-3 (sc)
ISBN: 978-1-4808-6461-0 (hc)
ISBN: 978-1-4808-6459-7 (e)

Library of Congress Control Number: 2018912434

Print information available on the last page.

Archway Publishing rev. date: 12/13/2018

To Jennifer

ABOUT THE AUTHOR

Larry Levine is founder, editor and publisher of the online food magazine *Table Talk atLarrys.com* (www.tabletalkatlarrys.com).

He has authored hundreds of features about food and restaurants and estimates he has cooked at least thirty thousand meals during a lifetime of passion for all things food-related.

Levine also is one of California's premier political consultants. He has directed more than two hundred campaigns for candidates and ballot measures in seven states, with a winning record of 88 percent. Before entering the world of politics, he was a news reporter and editor for fifteen years.

Levine lives in Los Angeles with his wife, Jennifer. They have two sons and four grandchildren. He was born in Brooklyn, New York and moved to Los Angeles when he was ten years old. He's been a Dodger fan, an opera fan, and a devotee of the musical comedy stage since his childhood.

When not cooking, shopping for food, writing about food, dining in some great restaurant, or running someone's campaign for public office, Levine most likely will be found on a golf course or traveling with Jennifer.

IN LOVING MEMORY

NORMA LEVINE
My mother at age 25

MYRNA LEVINE
My sister at age 17

ELISA LEVINE KRUTE
My sister at age 17

ROSEMARY GOLDER
Jennifer's older sister

Norma, Myrna, and Elisa Levine all were breast cancer patients who died of different forms of cancer. Rosemary Golder died of leukemia at the age of fifteen.

In their memory, 100 percent of the net profits from the sale of this book will be donated to organizations devoted to prevention and treatment of breast cancer and leukemia.

CONTENTS

Introduction xiii
What Is "A Beautiful Woman"? xvii
Author's Note xix

1. She Made the Music Start 1
   Mom: *Jewish Home Cooking from the Old Country*

2. The Day the War Ended 39
   V-J Day: *Recipes from a Soda Fountain in Brooklyn*

3. Puppy Love 51
   Boys and Girls Together: *New York Pushcart Treats*

4. California, Here I Am 63
   The Quintero Family: *Mexican Recipes*

5. First Touch 83
   And Then We Danced: *Barbecue*

6. The Christian Missionary and the Kid
   from Brooklyn 97
   A Unique Bonding: *Recipes for Chinese Food*

7. Forever Seventeen 119
   Teenage Infatuation: *A Taste of Basque Culture*

8. Convertible Cars and Celebrity Bars 127
   The Bachelor Years: *Omelets and Other Breakfasts*

9. Marna's Time 141
   She Left, and I Was Changed:
   Dinners on the Sunset Strip

10. The Three-Hour Cup of Coffee 153
    Fifty Years Later and Going Strong:
    Recipes from Our Dinner Table

11. An Indomitable Spirit, An Incredible Survival 193
    Tillie Tooter, One of a Kind:
    A Feast from a Jewish Aunt's Kitchen

12. Immortality Is a Granddaughter 207
    She Called Me Granddad:
    Adult Dishes that the Kids Love

13. Judy 221
    Two Unforgettable Nights:
    Recipes from the Las Vegas Strip

14. La Divina 233
    A Lifetime of Musical Magic: *A Favorite Greek Dish*

15. Fantasies 241
    Through the Years: *Desserts*

16. Mothers and Daughters and Others 253
    Personal and Professional Fulfillment:
    Recipes from Around the Globe

Tips for Using these Recipes 301
Index of Recipes 305
Acknowledgments 311

INTRODUCTION

From the streets and playgrounds of Brooklyn, New York, to the Sunset Strip and the Las Vegas Strip, and at countless stops along the way, the women of Cooking for a Beautiful Woman honed the tastes and wrote the tales of the wonderful life I have known.

They were singers and secretaries, classmates and teachers, actresses and attorneys, mothers, daughters, granddaughters, friends, lovers and mentors. Together and separately, they wove a tapestry of smiles and tears and inspired the warm, funny, tender, and sweet stories that fill these pages. Some achieved fame and celebrity, and you will recognize them. Others you will meet for the first time. But all were memorable women, strong and independent women, intelligent women.

There was my mother, who was a big-band singer in the 1930s; an aunt, whose miraculous survival made headlines around the world; a teacher, who left China two weeks before the Communist takeover in 1949; and the daughter of an immigrant family from Mexico, who became my first girlfriend after our family moved to Los Angeles from Brooklyn. There was the love affair that was supposed to last a lifetime but didn't, and the one that continues to grow after fifty years. There was Maria Callas, my first opera obsession; Judy Garland, the most electric entertainer I've ever seen; and Peggy Fleming, the figure-skating champion, who captivated me the first time I saw her skate and later grew to heroic dimensions beyond the world of skating.

For each of the women whose stories are told in these pages, there are recipes appropriate to the time and place she filled: old-country Romanian dishes handed down from my grandmother to my mother and then to me; recipes for Mexican, Chinese, Japanese, Basque, and Greek dishes; Jewish home cooking; New York soda fountain and pushcart recipes from the 1940s; and a few from one of Los Angeles' most revered Sunset Strip restaurants.

My affinity for food and the kitchen started simply. The first thing I ever cooked was a Boston cream pie. I was fourteen years old. My parents and sisters had gone to visit relatives on a Sunday afternoon in the fall of 1953 and I hadn't felt like going with them. Instead, I spent a few hours playing touch football at the park around the corner from our house. When I got home, I felt the urge to cook something. *Why* will forever be a mystery. It never happened before.

I found the recipe among others in a drawer in the kitchen. I went to the market, bought the ingredients, came home and made a perfect pie. I set it on the counter and waited to see what would happen. That's where Mom found it when she began to make dinner. "Where did this come from?" she asked.

The big smile on my face grew even broader later, after we had eaten the pie and everyone raved about it. Mom told me she had tried the same recipe a few times and thrown the pie away each time because it didn't turn out right. When I went to make a Boston cream pie several months later, the recipe had vanished. It became a running joke in the family, with me teasing my mother about "losing" the recipe that worked for me but not for her.

That innocent pie was how it started, but the real cooking began about a year later. My mother wasn't a great cook, although there were some things she cooked exceptionally well. Her gefilte fish was matchless. No one ever made a better chicken soup, mushroom-barley-beef soup, *kreplach* (dumplings), *lokshen kugel* (noodle pie), pickled lox, or pickled herring.

Spaghetti in red sauce, however, meant opening a can of tomato sauce, heating it, and pouring it over the pasta. Dessert was canned peaches, pears, or fruit cocktail. Liver was cooked to the consistency of what one would imagine a baseball glove or shoe leather might taste like, because that's how Dad preferred it. Ultimately, I told Mom I didn't want to have liver anymore. Rather than ask her to make a separate dinner for me, I said I would cook my own meals on the nights when she was making liver. The first time I did that I made calf's heart and mashed potatoes for myself. It was something Mom made for the family on occasion and I particularly liked. She gave me the money and I went to the market and bought the heart. My two sisters said they didn't like the liver either and asked if I would cook for them on the nights when Mom was making liver for Dad. Among the things I recall making are salami and eggs, baked chicken legs, and broiled lamb chops – simple stuff like that. As time went by, I became more adventurous.

That was some sixty-four years ago. I figure I've cooked somewhere in excess of thirty thousand meals since then. There have been holiday dinner parties for as many as twenty-five people and hundreds of breakfasts and dinners for Jennifer and me after our two sons moved out. There were the kitchen ballets I danced with dates in their apartments or mine as we prepared dinners together during my bachelor years, and there have been countless meals I've served to my sons, their wives, and our grandchildren.

There are few passions that rival food and cooking in my everyday life. A supermarket is like a playground, a place at which I chat with other customers, trade recipes and talk about food preparation. Restaurants are new frontiers to be sought and explored. And my kitchen is where I go to relax and play out some of my most creative instincts.

There is a certain irony that I'm sure Mom and Dad would appreciate about me becoming the editor and publisher of an internationally read online food magazine. I was born with what at the time was referred to as a shutdown, inverted stomach. The medical term is gastric volvulus. When I was a kid, my parents told me only three babies in medical history had survived that condition before I did. After three days of not being able to take in food, my stomach righted itself and I became the first person to survive the condition without surgery. Later, my father joked that I spent the rest of my life trying to make up for those three missed days of eating.

That survival was the beginning of the good fortune that has followed me through nearly eight decades. I have been fortunate to find success in three different careers: first as a newspaper and wire service reporter and editor, second as a political consultant, and third as a food writer and editor.

However, there has been no greater good fortune than having Jennifer enter my life and decide to stay. Our journey has exceeded any expectations I could have had when we met. Through the years, there has grown an abiding love, two remarkable sons, two wonderful daughters-in-law and four grandchildren, who make me want to never stop breathing even as they take my breath away.

I feel particularly fortunate that I never suffered from the "girls-are-yukky" affliction that infects so many preteen boys. For, from my earliest years, most of my best and most trusted friends have been girls and women. This book is my homage to them all, to the defining impact they have had in shaping the wonderful life I've enjoyed, and to the hundreds of memorable meals we've shared.

—Larry Levine

WHAT IS "A BEAUTIFUL WOMAN"?

I heard a radio report not long ago about a study in which the majority of men said the sexiest trait in a woman is her independence.

I've been around too long to buy that. I spent time in fraternity houses in college and locker rooms when I was a sports writer. Never once did I hear some guy say, "Did you see the independence on that blonde at the bar last night."

It got me thinking, however, about the subject in the context of the title of this book. *Am I objectifying women by referring to them as beautiful?* I wondered. *Am I reinforcing society's worst tendencies and sending the wrong messages to young girls, my granddaughters included? Do I have a responsibility to offer some thoughts or maybe an explanation?*

I hadn't considered it before I heard that radio report, but independence is a dominant trait among the women in this book. Jennifer, my wife, left her family in England to come to the United States at the age of twenty-two, with the intention of emigrating to Australia. Marna, who was an earlier love interest, left her family in Wisconsin and moved to Los Angeles in her early twenties. My mother walked away from a potential career as a professional singer to marry and raise a family. Tillie Tooter became a war widow in 1944 and raised her daughter as a single mom. Elizabeth Blackstone was a Christian missionary in China during the rise of communism. Others have run for and served in elected office, achieved remarkable success in the legal arena, or made their marks in other important ways.

I first went to work as a reporter in the press room of the

state capitol in 1965. A friend asked me recently what I believe is the biggest change in government and politics since that time. Without hesitation I answered, "The role of women. When I first got there, women were secretaries and receptionists. Now they are legislators and statewide office holders, chiefs-of staff, and heads of departments."

Independence lies in the character and life of the individual. That's what marks the women in this book: their intelligence, wit, and independence. Those are the things that define their beauty.

AUTHOR'S NOTE

In preparing this memoir, I have stuck to the facts as best I can recall them. If I've strayed here and there, remember, I've been gathering wonderful memories for 79 years and they all are crowded into the limited space of my cranium. You can take some confidence in the accuracy of the times, places and events related in these stories from the number of times people have said to me, "How in the world can you remember that?" Most deviations are the unintentional consequence of the fallacy of human memory. A few are placed intentionally to protect the privacy of the people involved. All of the people in this memoir were and are real, although I have used aliases for some, also to protect their privacy.

Among those for whom fictitious names are substituted for the real names are

Chapter 2: Rosie
Chapter 3: Stanley, Frances, Beth, Howard, Sally, Carol, and Gary
Chapter 4: Yolanda Quintero, Beth, Sally, Carol, Don, and Mrs. Quintero
Chapter 5: Linda
Chapter 6: Bill
Chapter 7: Phil, Dave, Rich, Barbara, and Lynne
Chapter 8: Jim and Brian
Chapter 16: Laurie Mattson

CHAPTER ONE
She Made the Music Start

NORMA AND PETER LEVINE
Mom and Dad on their wedding day in 1937. I was born two years later.

NORMA LEVINE
My mother during her days as a big-band singer under the stage name of Norma Stone.

It all started in the kitchen of a downstairs rear apartment in a two-story brick building in the Brownsville neighborhood of Brooklyn, New York, in the early 1940s.

The sounds and smells that filled that kitchen were the seeds that blossomed into the tastes I would develop and the passions I would come to know throughout my life. They were planted by the one woman who knew me longer than any other—Norma Anna Solomon Levine, my mother. She made the music start.

Mom was a big-band singer in the nightclubs of Manhattan in the 1930s. She performed under the stage name of Norma Stone. She stood five foot three, which led Broadway columnist Walter Winchell to call her "the little girl with the big voice." To be mentioned favorably in a Winchell column could make a career. But in 1937 Mom walked away from the Broadway nightlife to get married and raise a family. The notion that a woman could have it all was not widely accepted in those days before feminism took its place on the spectrum of broad public awareness. Many believed children of celebrity parents would be plagued with problems throughout their lives. Even today, real challenges confront women who choose both career and family—challenges that men don't face. Mom made her choice, and what a fortunate one it was for me. Two years later I became her firstborn.

My Brooklyn-born father, Peter Levine, left school at the age of eleven. Even at that young age, he was able to land a variety of jobs at circuses and carnivals that came through the New York area and on the Boardwalk at Coney Island. He spent most of his twenties in the Damon Runyonesque Broadway world of gamblers and bootleggers, and he was a regular at many of the nightclubs Mom frequented. That's where they met. When they decided to marry, Dad left that life behind. From then on, the skills he gained as a teenager at carnivals formed a big part of the foundation of his working life.

I remember clearly the many afternoons I spent sitting at the long, maple-wood table at one end of the large rectangular kitchen in our Brooklyn apartment. I would do my elementary school homework while Mom cooked or worked at her Singer sewing machine, singing all the while. She would belt out the damnedest Saint Louis Blues I've ever heard. Then the warmth and richness of her voice could make a heart smile as she sang the World War II hit "Anniversary Waltz". Her voice filled our home and our lives with popular songs from the twenties and thirties, English translations of old-country Yiddish and Jewish folk songs, Broadway show tunes, and new songs we heard together on the radio. She could hear a song once and remember the lyrics. I grew up thinking all mothers could sing like that.

In that kitchen in Brooklyn, Mom and I would listen to Metropolitan Opera broadcasts on our Philco tabletop radio most Saturday mornings during the opera season. Later, as an adult in Los Angeles, I would take her to dinner and the opera. Oh, the dozens of times she told me how she once saw Risé Stevens sing *Carmen* at the Hippodrome Theater on Sixth Avenue in Manhattan, ticket price twenty-five cents. To this day, I feel Mom beside me whenever I'm in an opera house or listening to an opera recording.

During my bachelor years, I took dates to the opera

whenever a touring company from New York or San Francisco visited Los Angeles, before we had our own opera company. It always was dinner first and then the theater. For most of my dates it was their first taste of opera. I've wondered often if any of them became fans—if they might be seated somewhere in the theater on a night when I'm there with Jennifer. Would I recognize them? Would they recognize me? Do they remember their first opera?

One of the women who saw her first opera with me was Jennifer. I can't begin to count the number of operas we've attended as we've marched through fifty years of life together. There's a path that runs directly from that kitchen in Brooklyn to opera houses in Los Angeles, San Francisco, New York, Milan, and Verona. Jennifer has traveled much of that path with me.

When Mom was eighty-five years old, she stayed with us for two weeks while recovering from something the doctors couldn't figure out during five days in the hospital. One Saturday morning, with the Southern California sun shining brightly and the doors and windows open to let in the warm spring air, Mom and I sat in our living room and listened to a Metropolitan Opera radio broadcast of *Tosca*. That afternoon, I took her to have her hair done. As we drove, we listened to Frank Sinatra on the car stereo and joined in to help him through "Pennies from Heaven" and "I Only Have Eyes for You." Later, while I was preparing dinner, Mom sat alone in the living room and sang "I Surrender Dear," which had been Bing Crosby's first solo hit. Her voice would dry out and crack occasionally, but it still was warm and big enough to bring tears to my eyes and Jennifer's.

"I Surrender Dear" was written by Harry Barris, who was one of orchestra leader Paul Whiteman's original Rhythm Boys, along with Bing Crosby and Al Rinker. When they were young and single, Harry and my father hung out at the same barbershop in Brooklyn, where they played cards and waited for the sun to set and the lights to come on over Broadway. Years later, Harry married Loyce Whiteman, a singer and daughter of Paul Whiteman. Harry and Loyce had a daughter, Marti, who was two years ahead of me in school in Burbank, California. We met in high school, but we didn't date until several years later. Marti forged her own career as a vocalist, actress, and songwriter. My father talked occasionally of contacting Harry, but he never did. Harry died in 1962, soon after Marti and I stopped dating. How's that for the randomness of the circle of life? My mother sang with Paul Whiteman's orchestra, and I dated his granddaughter thirty-plus years later, and she was the daughter of my dad's old friend from New York.

As the calendar continued to turn, Mom sang less and less, until finally she gave in to the constraints of ebbing health and stopped altogether. After singing her way through more than seven decades, how it must have hurt for her to say, "I can't do it anymore."

It was from Mom that I got an appreciation not just for opera and the songs of the big-band years but also for the likes of Jeanette MacDonald and Nelson Eddy and the great Broadway musicals. She took me to see *The Desert Song* when I was no more than six or seven years old. I have been hooked on the lore and magic of Broadway ever since—the perpetually young performers dancing and singing and acting and digging deep into their souls to entertain us. It's what made me an unapologetic romantic. Now I sit in theaters with my oldest granddaughter, Ella, watching musicals, and I know she is studying singing, dancing and acting and appearing in productions. I wish Mom could be there to see it. And how I wish Ella could have had a chance to hear her great-grandmother sing. What few recordings we had of Mom have long since disappeared.

If the music was Mom's greatest legacy, her passion for dining at fine restaurants, a taste she gained during her Broadway nightclub years, was a close second. She handed that on to me and my two late sisters. It now is securely vested in the lives of my two sons, each of whom loves to cook and feels comfortable in any kind of restaurant.

Just as the roots of my appreciation for great song lyrics are clear, there's no doubt my love of everything having to do with food—shopping for it, cooking it, eating it, writing about it—also comes directly from Mom. Early in my life, she introduced me to Maine lobster and clams on the half shell at Lundy's, the legendary seafood restaurant on Sheepshead Bay in Brooklyn. After we moved to Los Angeles, our family dined at places like the Oyster House and The Captain's Table on L.A.'s ritzy "Restaurant Row". It stretched the means of a working-class family, but we managed to afford them because they were important to Mom.

In 1996, after our son John's graduation from the University of Massachusetts at Amherst, Jennifer and I and the two boys—what else do you call your adult sons—took a vacation that led us to Maine, where we put a major dent in the local lobster population at a place called Nunan's Lobster Hut. True to its name, it was a shack of a place, with a red and white awning and picnic tables inside, right on the water in Cape Porpoise, just outside Kennebunkport. The menu offered only steamers (Ipswich clams), boiled lobster, and Maine wild blueberry pie. (They have expanded the menu since then.) The men in the family ran the lobster boats; the women ran the restaurant. If you ever get up that way, be sure to stop in. Lobster in Maine will spoil you for lobster anywhere else. Mom never got to Nunan's, but the thought of her attacking a lobster in that setting is a vision that puts a smile on my face. Mom confronted any lobster set before her with total devotion. Not a word was spoken until the last bite was consumed.

All these things that Mom gave to me ... they are at the top of the treasure chest that holds so many of my fondest memories. As early as high school, I went on dates other guys never considered. When the movie *Around the World in 80 Days* was released in 1956, I saw it over and over again, each time with a different date. We would go to dinner on "Restaurant Row" before heading for the magnificent Carthay Circle Theater. Mom would slip me a few dollars on the way out the door to supplement what I had earned from summer jobs working with Dad as an apprentice plumber. She loved that I was going to these places. She called it, with great affection, "cosmopolitan."

Most of my friends only *got dressed up* for the birthday of a steady girlfriend or some other special occasion. From Mom I learned there is no reason to reserve those pleasures for special occasions—they are special in themselves.

Mom died in the summer of 2001. She went in the one way she always said she didn't want to go. Mom told us often, "When the time comes, don't keep me around; just pull the plug and let me go; I don't want to lie around like a vegetable."

Sadly, that's just what wound up happening. Two years before she died, sapped of her strength and spirit by her latest bout with cancer, able to do little other than sit on the couch and read or watch television, Mom told me, "This is no way to live. I'm ready to go." But she couldn't. The law wouldn't allow it. Attempts to pass Death with Dignity laws in California had been blocked by pressure from the California Medical Association, religious groups, and disability-rights advocates. So she lingered there, helped to move between her couch, her bed, and the bathroom by my sister Elisa. When it became too much for Elisa to handle, we made the wrenching decision to move Mom to a nursing home. There, for eight months, she grew weaker and weaker. Physically, she was a shell, unable to care for herself; she languished in that sparse, pale green room in the most undignified way. Her lips might move, but no sound would come out.

Then, near the end, her younger sister, my late aunt Tillie, came to visit from her home in South Florida with her daughter, my cousin Linda. We tried to prepare Tillie and Linda for what they were going to find at that nursing home. The spirited woman with a robust voice and laugh was just a memory. Tillie talked to Mom but got no answer; that glorious voice had been silenced. Tillie held Mom's hand, knowing it would be the last time. Then, as it was nearing time to go, Tillie leaned close to Mom and sang a song from their youth. Mom looked at Tillie through clouded eyes, and in a voice stronger than anyone had heard for months, she joined in and together they sang

> *Now it's time for parting,*
> *and the tears are starting.*
> *Leave me with a smile.*

That was Mom's last song: "Leave Me with a Smile," sung with her sister in a nursing home a long, long way from the nightclubs of Broadway and our kitchen in Brooklyn.

I didn't cry when Mom died. Her death was a release from the indignity with which she had been living. But now, all these years later, there are times when tears do come, usually when I hear certain songs, ones she sang. On a road trip a few years ago, Jennifer and I played a recording of "With a Song in My Heart" on the car stereo. It's a song Mom sang a thousand times.

> *With a song in my heart*
> *I behold your adorable face;*
> *Just a song at the start,*
> *But it soon is a hymn to your grace …*
> *And I always knew*
> *I would live life through*
> *With a song in my heart for you.*

Jennifer took off her glasses and sobbed into a towel. I wiped the tears from beneath my sunglasses as I drove. For there is a song in my heart—the song Mom put there. And in that song and so many others, she always will be with us.

Mom's cooking consisted mostly of traditional Jewish and Romanian dishes handed down from her mother. Whether it was in Brooklyn or Los Angeles, the aromas of baked brisket, chicken soup, or herring and onions pickling in a gallon jar on the kitchen counter were as present in our home as were the sounds of Mom's songs. Sometimes I wonder if she might not have been able to cook if she hadn't been singing while doing it.

Though the sounds of her songs are gone, I keep the memories of her alive in the meals she prepared for us that I now prepare in my kitchen. Some of them have appeared in my son Lloyd's kitchen as well, when he cooks for his family and friends.

Mom cooked the way she learned from her Romanian mother – no recipes. If it looked right, smelled right, and tasted right, then it *was* right. That's the way I usually cook too. It's fulfilling to walk into the kitchen with no idea what we're having for dinner, open the refrigerator, peer into the pantry, pour a glass of wine, put something on the stereo, and get to work. No matter how many times I turn out delicious meals that way, it still amuses me. There must be something to this heredity stuff.

When I set out to write this book, I had to prepare all the old dishes and make notes to create recipes I could pass along to you. Instead of pouring some dried herb or spice into my hand, crushing it against my palm and dumping into the pot or pan, I had to use a measuring spoon, an implement with which previously I had only a passing relationship. I figured it out, but I learned that my favorite words when cooking are "to taste." That's what cooking is all about—"to taste."

The following are recipes for some of Mom's dishes that were handed down by word of mouth from my Romanian grandmother, through Mom, to me, and now to you. Some are written on 3" x 5" cards in Mom's own handwriting; most I had to recreate from having watched her or by remembering the taste of what she served for dinner.

Norma Levine's Chicken Soup

Every Jewish cook has his or her own recipe for what often is called "Jewish penicillin." Have a cold or the flu? Chicken soup. At home recovering from heart surgery? Chicken soup. First cold weather of the winter? Chicken soup to prevent colds and flu. Hangnail? Chicken soup. It isn't just a myth. There actually is medical research that proves it works. Mom's secret was the chicken feet. When I tell people Mom used necks, backs, gizzards, and feet in addition to the other parts of the chicken, I'm not surprised if the look I get back says they can't be bothered to try it. But I wouldn't think of doing it any other way. If you can't find chicken feet at your local supermarket and the butcher won't order them for you, try a local kosher butcher or an Asian supermarket.

> 1 fryer chicken, about 4 to 4 1/2 pounds
> 1 dozen chicken feet
> 1/2 pound chicken gizzards
> 6 chicken necks
> 4 chicken backs
> 1 large onion, quartered
> 2 celery stalks, cut into 1-inch pieces, plus extra leaves
> 2 large parsnips, scrubbed and cut in large chunks
> 6 large carrots, divided
> 3 bay leaves
> 1 tablespoon coarse kosher salt
> 4 quarts water, or more as needed to cover all the solids
> 1 (6-ounce) package fine egg noodles

Remove the large lumps of fat from the chicken. Cut the chicken into parts: legs, thighs, wings, breast halves, back. Put the chicken parts, feet, gizzards, necks, backs, onion, celery stalks and leaves, and parsnips in a 12-quart soup pot.

Scrub three of the carrots and cut them into 1-inch chunks and add them to the pot. Add the bay leaves and salt. Add at least four quarts of water to the pot—more if needed to cover the chicken and vegetables. Bring the water to a boil. Lower the heat to a slow boil for 2 hours.

With a slotted spoon, remove all the solids from the soup. Discard the chicken feet, bay leaves, and all the vegetables. Save the chicken legs and thighs, gizzards, and backs on a plate. Strain the soup and return it to the pot.

As for the necks, discard the skin and give yourself a treat: suck the juice from the ends and pick off and eat the meat. Then throw away the bones. (If you want to make a friend for life of your cat, give him or her the breast and neck meat for dinner.)

Put the pot of soup in the refrigerator for 24 hours. Cover the chicken and gizzards on a plate with plastic wrap, and put them in the refrigerator.

The next day, skim the fat from the top of the soup. Heat the soup over low heat. Peel the remaining three carrots, slice them into 1/4-inch rings, and put them into the soup. Strip the meat from the legs, thighs, and backs, and add it to the soup in small pieces. Cut the gizzards into halves and add them to the soup. Cook the soup at a slow boil for 30 minutes.

Taste the soup and add more salt if necessary.

Prepare the egg noodles according to the package directions.

To serve, put a generous amount of noodles in the bottom of a bowl. Ladle the soup with chicken and carrots over the noodles.

Note: Many people and most delis use the breast meat as well as the dark meat in the soup. I find the white meat too dry and lacking in taste, although the cat seems to like it.

In addition to sucking the juice out of the necks, Mom loved to suck on the chicken feet before tossing them out.

This should give you about ten hefty bowls of soup when you include the matzo balls.

Matzo Balls (Knaidlach)

Mom used seltzer from the old-fashioned pressurized bottles. It makes the matzo balls light and airy. It's hard to find those seltzer bottles these days. Instead, I use the most highly carbonated, unflavored water I can find. Perrier works well. So does club soda.

> 3 eggs
> about 3/4 cup seltzer water
> 2 1/2 ounces melted chicken fat
> 3/4 cup matzo meal
> 1/2 teaspoon salt
> 1/4 teaspoon finely ground black pepper (or more to taste)
> 3 quarts water, lightly salted

Beat the eggs with a whisk until they are light and frothy. Add all the ingredients to the eggs and mix together thoroughly. Cover with plastic wrap and let stand at least two hours in the refrigerator. Bring the salted water to a boil. Form the matzo meal mixture into balls with a soup spoon. Drop the balls gently into the boiling water, taking care to avoid overcrowding. (Matzo balls will expand as they cook.) Cook for about 1/2 hour at a moderate boil, until the matzo balls are cooked through and any sign of uncooked mixture is gone. (I find it helps to turn the matzo balls over in the water, using a slotted spoon, for the last 10 minutes.)

Some help: If you cannot find chicken fat at your local butcher shop, try a kosher butcher. If that doesn't work, substitute a vegetable oil. If you have to make this change, then add 1 tablespoon of onion powder or granulated onion to the mixture. You can make your own chicken fat by frying chicken skins in a skillet. Pour the liquified fat into a jar and refrigerate.

(After the matzo balls are done, you will find cooked batter floating in the water. For a treat, drain it, add a little salt and pepper, and eat it with a spoon.)

Old-Country Beef, Barley, and Mushroom Soup

After making this soup for what may have been the hundredth time, I'm still surprised by how easy it is and how wonderfully complex are the flavors. It's a real stick-to-the-bones dinner at the end of a chilly or rainy day.

> 1 pound beef marrow bones
> 1 1/2 pounds beef flanken ribs cut into pieces of 2 or 3 bones each
> 2 1/2 quarts water
> 1 celery stalk, cut in 1-inch pieces, with extra leaves
> 1 onion, diced
> 2 teaspoons salt
> 1/2 teaspoon black pepper
> 1/2 teaspoon powdered ginger
> 2 packages (1/2-ounce each) dried porcini mushrooms, soaked to soften according to package directions
> 3/4 cup pearl barley
> 5 white mushrooms, quartered
> 1 cup diced carrots

Wash the bones under cold water to remove any slivers and fragments from the butcher's saw. Place the marrow bones, flanken, and the next six ingredients in a large soup pot. Make sure there's enough water to cover all the other ingredients. Cover the pot and bring the water to a boil. Reduce the heat and cook at a slow boil for 2 hours. Remove the bones and meat. Set the flanken aside to cool. Strain the liquid and discard all the other solids.

(At this point it's a good idea to cover the broth and refrigerate it overnight so the fat will congeal and can be removed easily before proceeding.)

When the flanken has cooled, remove the meat from the bones, pull the meat apart into small pieces and return it to the soup. Bring the soup to a boil, and add the barley and soaked porcini mushrooms. Simmer for 2 more hours. Add the carrots and white mushrooms and simmer another 1/2 hour.

Makes about ten bowls of soup. Two bowls are good for a dinner entrée on a chilly night. I usually double this recipe and freeze a few portions.

Navy Bean Soup

My father introduced me to Navy bean soup at the old Horn & Hardart's Automat in Manhattan. Navy bean soup and baked beans were his favorites at the Automat. We would slide our coin into the slot, open the glass door and take out our bowl of soup or beans. Mom made Navy bean soup at home and used beef bones instead of a ham shank. I prefer the smokiness of the shank, but either will work well. If you use beef bones you probably will want to add more salt.

> 1 pound dried Navy beans (or substitute great northern beans)
> water
> 1 large, meaty smoked ham shank
> 3 medium russet potatoes, peeled and diced
> 1 large onion, chopped
> 1 cup diced celery
> 1 cup diced carrots
> 2 garlic cloves, minced
> salt and pepper to taste

Soak the beans overnight in enough water to cover them by about two inches. The next day add two more quarts of water and the ham shank. Cover the pot, bring the water to a boil, reduce the heat and simmer for 2 hours.

Add the potatoes, onion, celery, carrot and garlic. Simmer for an additional hour. Remove the ham shank from the pot and set it aside to cool. Run the soup through a Foley grinder (food mill), put it in a blender, or use an immersion blender to turn the whole thing into a nice thick soup. Cover the pot and put it in the refrigerator overnight so the fat will congeal and can be skimmed easily.

When the shank has cooled, strip the meat, cover it with plastic wrap and refrigerate.

When you are ready to serve the soup, return the ham to the pot and heat the soup. Stir frequently over medium-low heat to avoid burning the bottom. Add salt and pepper to taste. The ham will have given the soup a nice saltiness, so you may not need to add any.

This makes about 4 quarts of soup. It can be frozen in individual portions.

Sweet-and-Sour Russian Cabbage Soup

This recipe recalls the heritage of my father's side of the family. Both of his parents came to the United States from Russia in the late 1800s.

> 1 (28-ounce) can diced tomatoes
> 6 cups water
> 3 pounds flanken ribs
> 2 soup bones (neck or knuckle bones will work)
> 1 (6-ounce) can tomato paste
> 1 large head cabbage (about 2 pounds), coarsely shredded
> 2 tablespoons coarse salt
> 3/4 cup dry red wine
> juice 1 lemon
> 1/2 teaspoon cayenne pepper
> 1/2 teaspoon paprika

In a large stockpot, combine the tomatoes and water and bring them to a boil. Rinse the flanken and soup bones well to remove any bone chips. Cut the flanken into sections of 2 or 3 bones each. Add the flanken, the soup bones and all the other ingredients to the pot.* Stir to mix thoroughly. Bring to a boil. Reduce the heat and simmer, covered, for 2 1/2 hours.

Remove the flanken and soup bones. Discard the soup bones. Trim the flanken from the bones, tear the meat into small pieces and return the meat to the soup. Let the soup cool. Skim any fat from the top. If you have the time, refrigerate the soup overnight so the fat will congeal and be easier to remove. Reheat to serve.

Serve with small green salad or pumpernickel bread.

Here's a tip: Count the number of flanken bones you put into the pot. It's very likely the meat will cook off some of the bones. It will help to know how many you are trying to fish out of the pot when the time comes.

Makes eight hefty portions.

Romanian Eggplant Salad

From Mom's side of the family comes this dish that can be served as a first-course salad or as a dip before dinner. Even people who say they don't like eggplant attack this dip with vigor. My son Lloyd is one such person. He doesn't like eggplant but called me for this recipe the first time he wanted to make it for a dinner party at his home. I've seen similar dishes offered on menus as "eggplant caviar."

> 1 eggplant, about 1 pound
> 1/4 cup finely chopped onion
> 2 medium tomatoes, cut into small pieces
> 1 tablespoon olive oil (or to taste)
> 2 teaspoons lemon juice (or to taste)
> 12 Greek-style black olives, pitted and quartered
> salt to taste

Preheat the oven to 400 degrees. Wash and dry the eggplant. Pierce the skin of the eggplant in several places with the point of a knife to prevent it from exploding in the oven. Place it in a shallow baking dish and bake the eggplant for 40 minutes.

Let the eggplant cool. Use a spoon to scrape the flesh from the skin into a bowl. Chop the eggplant thoroughly with the edge of the spoon. Put the chopped eggplant in a fine strainer and let the juice drain. Return the eggplant to the bowl. Mix the onions and tomatoes into the chopped eggplant. Stir in the olive oil and lemon juice to taste. Stir in the olives. Add salt to taste. Cover and refrigerate until about 30 minutes before you are ready to serve.

Uncover the eggplant and let it stand at room temperature. Mix before serving. Taste again at room temperature and add salt if needed. Remember, the olives will be very salty, so use care in adding salt. If you omit the olives you will need to use more salt.

As a dip, serve this with plain water crackers or sesame crackers.

As a first-course salad, this should be enough for 6 to 8 people. Serve it on a leaf of butter lettuce.

Pickled Lox

Lox is fully "cooked" as brined salmon. Most frequently it is served as a sandwich on a bagel with cream cheese, tomato, and onion. Mom would transform lox into this wonderful lunch.

> 2-pound piece of belly lox
> 1 1/2 cups white vinegar
> 1/2 teaspoon vegetable oil
> 1/4 teaspoon sugar
> 1 1/2 cups water
> 2 very large brown onions, sliced thinly
> 4 laurel bay leaves
> 4 small red chili peppers, cut in half lengthwise and seeds removed
> 2 tablespoons whole black peppercorns

Cut the lox into cubes of about 1 1/2 inch each.

Bring the vinegar to a boil. Add the vegetable oil, sugar and water. Stir to dissolve the sugar. Remove the mixture from the heat and allow it to cool completely. You don't want to cook the lox by using warm or hot vinegar.

Put a layer of the lox pieces on the bottom of a glass jar. Then put a layer of sliced onion on top of the lox. Put one chili pepper, one bay leaf and about 1/4 teaspoon of black peppers on top of the onion. Repeat this layering until all ingredients are used. Pour the vinegar over the layers, cover the jar and let it stand in the refrigerator for three days.

That's all there is to it. You'll have a great lunch, with corn rye bread, buttered if you like.

Makes about eight lunch-size portions.

Potato Latkes Dad's Way

This was a team effort: Dad would prepare the latke mixture, Mom would do the frying. When Dad started making this, there were no in-home kitchen blenders or food processors. He used the fine side of an old-fashioned box grater. It was more romantic his way. I use my electric blender. It feels like cheating, but the latkes come out just fine, and my arm feels a lot better when I'm finished.

> 1 pound russet potatoes
> 1 medium brown onion
> 1 large egg, lightly beaten
> matzo meal as needed
> 1/4 teaspoon salt
> 1/4 teaspoon ground black pepper
> vegetable oil for frying

Peel and grate the potatoes—either Dad's way, by hand, or on the grate setting of a blender or food processor. Put batches of the grated potatoes in cold water as you go to prevent them from discoloring. When all the potatoes are grated, let them soak in the water about 2 more minutes, then drain them very well. Place in a mixing bowl. Grate the onion and stir it into the potatoes. Add the egg to the potato and onion mixture.

You are going to want the mixture to be moist but not runny. If it's too watery mix in some matzo meal until you get a consistency that will stand frying. You don't want it too dry, either, or it will fall apart. Stir in the salt and pepper.

Heat 1/4 cup of vegetable oil to medium-high in a wide frying pan. Don't let it start to smoke.*

You will want about 2 tablespoons of the potato mixture per latke, and the latkes should be fairly thin. Reduce the heat to medium. Drop spoonsful of the mixture into the hot oil, and use a spatula to flatten into rounds of about 2 1/2 inches each. Fry until the undersides are browned, about 5 minutes. Turn the latkes over and fry until the second side is browned, about 5 more minutes. Remove the latkes from the pan and place them on paper towels to drain the oil. Add more oil to the pan as needed, and skim off fried bits of potato left in the pan before adding more of the mixture.

To keep the latkes warm while you make additional batches, after draining, put the latkes on a wire rack in a shallow baking pan and put them in a preheated oven at 250 degrees.

Makes fourteen to sixteen latkes.

*Extra virgin *olive oil will not heat enough without smoking. Use lighter olive oil or some other kind of oil that doesn't have a strong taste.*

Serve with apple sauce and/or sour cream, or just serve the latkes as a side with a tri-tip roast,

Lokshen Kugel (Noodle Pie)

In most Jewish households, a kugel is a baked pudding or casserole. The base usually is potatoes or egg noodles. To that, all manner of things have been added—things like apples, carrots, cheeses, broccoli, spinach, pineapple, or even caramel. My mother preferred a straightforward egg-noodle pie fried on the stovetop. She would serve this most frequently with some kind of roast beef or steak.

> 1 (8-ounce) package of egg noodles
> 3 eggs, beaten
> salt and pepper to taste
> 1/4 cup oil for frying

Prepare the noodles in boiling water as per package directions. Do not overcook them. You want them cooked but firm.

Drain the noodles very well. Mix in the beaten eggs. Heat the oil in a wide frying pan. Add the noodles and spread them evenly in the pan. Fry over medium-high heat until the noodles are well browned to a crispy crust. Turn the pie over and fry the second side until well browned. Remove the pie to paper towels to absorb any extra oil.

To serve, cut the pie into wedges.

Stuffed Cabbage

Mom made stuffed cabbage frequently. It was one of Dad's favorites. When I decided to make it for the first time, I asked Mom for her recipe. She said she didn't have one. Then she recited a list of ingredients, along with approximate proportions. For the rest, I had to trust my memory and instincts. This is the result.

> 1 large head of cabbage
> 1 tablespoon butter or olive oil
> 1 brown onion, sliced and divided
> 1 pound ground beef, fat content 15% or less
> 4 tablespoons cooked long-grain white rice
> water
> 1 teaspoon salt, divided
> 1/2 teaspoon black pepper, divided
> 1 (8-ounce) can tomato sauce
> 1/4 cup seedless golden raisins
> 3 tablespoons honey
> 1 tablespoon lemon juice

Peel 8 large outer leaves from the cabbage and trim away the thick stems. Steam the leaves quickly until crisp tender, just a minute or two. Melt the butter in a frying pan. Add half the onions and sauté until they are lightly browned. Add the ground beef, cooked rice, 4 tablespoons water, 1/2 teaspoon salt and 1/4 teaspoon black pepper. Stir and cook over medium-high heat until the beef is browned and crumbly.

Place meat mixture on each cabbage leaf, according to the size of the leaf. Tuck in the ends of the leaves. Roll the leaves and secure with a wooden toothpick. Combine the tomato sauce, 1 cup of water, remaining onion, salt and black pepper. Arrange the cabbage rolls in a baking dish with the seam side down, and pour the tomato sauce mixture over the rolls. Cover and bake at 350 degrees for one hour.

Add the raisins, honey and lemon juice. Cook, uncovered 30 minutes longer.

Serves eight.

Beef with Noodles and Cheese

> 2 healthy handfuls of broad egg noodles
> 1 tablespoon olive oil
> 2 slices red onion, diced
> 1 pound ground beef, fat content 15% or less
> 1 1/2 tablespoons plus 1/4 cup grated Romano cheese, divided
> dash of Worcestershire sauce
> dash of Tabasco sauce
> 1 teaspoon dried oregano, divided
> 4 tablespoons tomato sauce
> 4 tablespoons ricotta cheese
> 1/4 cup each shaved Jack and cheddar cheeses

Boil the noodles 15 minutes in salted water. Drain and set aside.

Heat the olive oil in a 10-inch frying pan. Sauté the onions in the oil, stirring frequently, until softened.

Mix together the beef, 1 1/2 tablespoons of Romano cheese, Worcestershire sauce, Tabasco sauce, and 1/2 teaspoon of oregano. Add the mixture to the onions and cook, stirring frequently, until the meat is lightly browned.

Mix together the tomato sauce, ricotta cheese and remaining 1/2 teaspoon of oregano. Add this to the ground beef. Cook until the beef is cooked through and well heated.

Spread the noodles on the bottom of a 7" x 10" casserole or similar size. Spread the beef mixture over the noodles. Sprinkle with the remaining Romano cheese. Top with the

Jack and cheddar cheeses. Bake, uncovered, 15 minutes in a preheated oven at 350 degrees.

Serve with a green salad.

Makes four portions, or skip the salad and it makes two large portions.

Norma Levine's Gefilte Fish
(Handwritten version)

I have a piece of note paper with Mom's gefilte fish recipe in her own handwriting. Unfortunately, it's too faded to reproduce here. What follows is the recipe exactly as she wrote it—with her own unique spelling, abbreviations, and lack of punctuation. It's the same recipe her mother brought to the U.S. from Romania in the late 1800s, although I have no reason to believe my great-grandmother ever wrote it down.

My late sister Elisa and I had this recipe to work with when we decided to make gefilte fish for a holiday dinner the year after Mom died. We had been around the house often enough while Mom was making gefilte fish to have picked up additional information to fill in the blanks, and we knew her well enough to interpret some of the things in this recipe.

> 1 medium size white fish
> 1 medium size yellow pike
> 1 medium size sucker
> 1 small size buffalo (fish)
> 3-inch slice of (*shpegal*) carp

ask man to fillet & save all skins bones & heads ask man for extra carp head
4 large onions 3 eggs 3 1/2 tables koshering salt 4 large carrots 1 1/2 teas peper 3/4 cup seltzer (or water)
put skins & carp head aside in 3 cups of water
cook bones & other heads with 1 of the onions 1/2 tables salt & 1/2 teas peper 1 1/2 hrs

stew 3 onions in 1/2 teas oil until very dark brown but not burned.

strain juice from bones in large pot add skin & carp head & sliced 3 1/2 carrots cover & simmer grind onions add 1 heaping tables to juice simmer

grind all fish to rest of onions mix, grind again add 1/2 ground carrot eggs rest of salt & peper 1/4 cup seltzer

mix well add 1/4 cup seltzer mix again

if hands come clean with no fish sticking to hands do not add remaining seltzer. If fish sticks to hand add remaining seltzer make medium size patties

line pot fish should not touch one another cook 10 min, shake pot slowly add another layer of fish cook 10 more min, Shake pot slowly continue this until all fish is in pot simmer 1/2 hour —add 2 ounce water shake pot, repeat this until fish cooks 1 1/2 hrs

Norma Levine's Gefilte Fish
(user-friendly translation)

Here's the same recipe as I translated it from Mom's original. This is a difficult and challenging dish, but you'll wallow in the praise that accompanies every bite. You'll never again be able to eat the stuff that comes in a jar, and you'll be hard pressed to match it in any restaurant.

> 1 medium whole white fish
> 1 medium whole yellow pike
> 1 medium whole sucker
> 1 small whole buffalo (fish)
> 3-inch slice of (*shpegal*) carp
> 3 cups water
> 4 large onions, divided
> 3 1/2 tablespoons koshering salt, divided
> 1 1/2 teaspoons ground black pepper, divided
> 1/4 cup light olive oil
> 1 carp head
> 4 large carrots, divided
> 3 eggs
> 3/4 cup seltzer water or carbonated water

Ask the fishmonger to skin and fillet the fish, saving the skins, bones and heads. Put the skins and carp head aside.

Put all the bones and other heads in a pot with 3 cups of water, along with one of the onions, quartered, 1/2 teaspoon each salt and pepper. Simmer for 1 1/2 hours.

In the meantime, heat the oil in a wide frying pan. Slice three onions and cut them into half-moons. Stew the onions in the oil until very dark brown but not burned. (See stewing directions below.)

Strain the liquid from the bones into a large pot and discard the bones. Add the skins, carp head, and three-and-a-half carrots that are sliced in quarter-inch rounds. Cover and bring to a simmer.

Grind the stewed onions in a food mill, or mash them well with a fork. Add a heaping tablespoon of the stewed onion to the pot with the liquid, skins, and carp head. Simmer for 1 1/2 hours.

Grind all the fish and the rest of the stewed onions. Mix with your hands to incorporate the onions with the fish. Then grind it again.

Grind the remaining half carrot and add it to the fish along with the eggs, the rest of the salt and pepper, and 1/2 cup of seltzer. Mix well with your hands. Add another 1/4 cup seltzer and mix again with your hands. If your hands come out with no fish sticking to them, do not add the remaining seltzer. If the fish sticks to your hands, add the remaining seltzer and mix again.

Form the ground fish mixture into medium-size balls. Put the fish balls into the pot with the hot liquid. The fish balls should not touch each other. Simmer 10 minutes.

Shake the pot gently. Add another layer of fish balls. Cook 10 more minutes. Shake the pot gently again; continue to add the fish and shake the pot until all the fish is in the pot. Simmer 1/2 hour.

Add two ounces of water. Shake the pot gently and simmer. Shake the pot occasionally and continue to simmer until the fish is cooked—about 1 1/2 hours.

Remove the fish and the carrot slices from the pot. Arrange them on a platter, cover it with plastic wrap, and put it in the refrigerator.

Strain the liquid in which the fish was cooked. Pour it into a jar or serving bowl, cover it, and put it in the refrigerator.

Remove the fish from the refrigerator about 1/2 hour before serving. Serve with sliced carrots and the jarred fish broth, which will have turned to a jelly.

Serve with a side of prepared horseradish (recipe follows).

You should have enough fish balls for a first course for a modest-size dinner party of eight to ten people.

STEWING THE ONIONS
To stew the onions: sauté the onion slices in the oil until they are well softened and just beginning to brown at the edges. Add 1/2 cup of tap water, turn the heat down and cover the pan. Check the onions occasionally, stirring to be sure they don't burn. Add more water as needed, and stew until dark brown. This is going to take a fair amount of time.

Horseradish for Gefilte Fish

Be careful—very, very careful. This stuff is hot. Wash your hands well with soap a few times when you finish. Whatever you do, don't touch your eyes. Keep a batch of tissues close by, because your nose and eyes will run. When eating the horseradish, be very careful. This stuff is hot.

> 1 red beet, peeled
> 2 tablespoons white vinegar
> 1/2 teaspoon sugar
> 1 tablespoon water
> 1 piece of horseradish, 4 inches long

Boil the beet until it is soft, 30 to 40 minutes. Cut the beet into small to medium pieces. Put it in a blender with the vinegar, sugar, and water. Grate the beet, but do not liquefy. Strain the beet and save the juice. Discard the pulp.

Peel the horseradish. If you are ambitious, you may want to grate the horseradish by hand on a box grater the way my Dad used to do it. Otherwise, chop the horseradish into small pieces. Put it in a blender and grate it to a coarse texture. Then stir the beet juice into the horseradish.

Be careful. This horseradish mixture is going to be very hot. That's one of the many great reasons to serve the fish and horseradish with a nice, fresh sliced challah.

Refrigerate the horseradish until about 15 minutes before serving. It will keep in the refrigerator for weeks in a lidded jar, although I've never found another use for it besides with the gefilte fish.

CHAPTER TWO

The Day the War Ended

VJ DAY
Celebrations erupted across the nation on VJ Day, the day Japan surrendered to end WW II in August, 1945. Nowhere were the festivities grander than on the streets of Brooklyn.

RATION BOOK
Mom would send me around the corner to Abie's Grocery Store or Harry's Butcher Shop in Brooklyn during the war. Using ration cards like this, I would bring home what she ordered, and she would pay them later.

WAR DEPARTMENT TELEGRAM
What a relief. There would be no more telegrams like this one from the War Department telling another wife or mother of the death of a loved one. We could go back to being "just kids" in the neighborhoods.

*B*etween the end of The War—World War II—and the end of innocence, there were the years of living well. For me, this was in Brooklyn in the late 1940s—a time before fear of people with a different color skin drove longtime residents to flee the borough. It was a time when kids were allowed to roam the neighborhoods and shape their own relationships, a time before "play dates" and overprotective adult intrusion into young imaginations.

Kids grew up early on the streets of Brooklyn in the 1940s, not because of gangs, turf wars, and drugs but because of the freedom that came with the postwar euphoria. On summer afternoons, when I was just eight years old, my parents would allow me to go to Brooklyn Dodger baseball games at Ebbets Field without adult supervision. With a dollar in my pocket and a group of friends around me, I would climb the steps to the elevated train platform, ride the few stops to the Grand Army Plaza subway station, walk to the ballpark, buy a ticket for a seat in the second deck of the center-field bleachers, and buy a score card, a hot dog, a drink, and a bag of peanuts. After the game, we kids would hang out at the players' entrance and wait for our heroes to come out—Gil (Hodges) and Pee Wee (Reese) and Jackie (Robinson) and Campy (Roy Campanella) and Duke (Snider) and Newk (Don Newcombe) and all the rest. They would stand on the sidewalk and sign autographs and talk with us. Sometimes we would walk them to their cars or the entrance to the subway station or the nearby barber shop, where they played cards before heading for home. We knew to not bother a player who had a bad day at the ball park and to be sensitive if they lost that day's game. Our subway ride home took another nickel and at the end of the day I would be left with five cents to keep.

In 1947 a young man named Jackie Roosevelt Robinson rode into town from California. We were eight and nine-year-old kids and Jackie's race meant nothing to us. It was only the adults who talked about things like that. To us he was Jackie—just Jackie—and all that mattered was that we believed he would help our Dodgers beat the hated Giants for the National League pennant and the hated Yankees in the World Series. Jackie was going to mean the difference between victory and continued frustration. He represented the optimistic future that was going to chase away the shadow that hung over our heavily Jewish neighborhood and most of the rest of the nation in the first half of the 1940s, when even on the brightest of days there was the ever-present shadow of war. We couldn't have imagined there would be eight more years of futility before Jackie and our Dodgers finally did win a World Series. Before all those wonderful days, however, there was the war.

I was six years old when Germany surrendered to end the war in Europe and Japan surrendered to end the war in the Pacific. I remember air-raid sirens and searchlights that cut through the dark night skies. I remember my parents telling me it was to protect us in case German bombers came across the ocean to attack us. No child should have to go to bed every night thinking about things like that, whether it be in Brooklyn in the 1940s or in Israel, Aleppo, or other places around the world today.

I remember air-raid wardens visiting our apartment. They reminded us to keep the window shades down after dark and to seal any cracks that might allow light to be seen by enemy pilots. They told us we should turn off all lights when the sirens sounded because that might mean enemy planes were approaching. I wondered how turning off the lights in our apartment would help if they were going to shine those searchlights in the air. Wouldn't those great beams of light tell the enemy where we were?

I remember tests of the sirens every Friday at noon. I thought that if I were the Germans I would send the bombers at noon on Friday, when everyone would think it was just a test.

Even in those difficult times, there were many Saturday mornings when my father and I would walk up the slope to the end of our block, cross the street, pass a row of shops and restaurants, and cross under the elevated train tracks to reach the Sutter Theater. Along the way, we would stop for a lime rickey and perhaps a hot dog or hero sandwich. At the theater we would see a double feature, maybe *The Lone Ranger*, or *Hopalong Cassidy*, or some other western. There were cartoons and often a Superman serial. There also was the Fox Movietone newsreel, which brought us pictures of the war and reports from the front.

I remember how, when we fried bacon at home—yes, bacon in our Jewish household—we saved the rendered fat in a coffee can. Mom took the cans of congealed fat somewhere to help the war effort. I couldn't figure out how bacon fat would help. We also saved rubber bands, used tinfoil, string, and newspapers, which we gave to the scrap man who visited the neighborhood in his beat-up truck once a week, again collecting for the war effort. Years later I learned a pound of bacon fat contains enough glycerin to make about one pound of explosives.

I remember Mom tearing small stamps from ration books and giving them to me when she sent me around the corner to the grocery store or butcher shop with a shopping list. I remember Victory Gardens on empty lots, where people from the neighborhood grew vegetables, and I remember bringing empty wooden cheese boxes to school, planting carrot seeds in them, and then taking the boxes home to nurture the seeds until they became food for our table.

I remember the radio programs that featured popular singers and comedians, who urged us to buy war bonds.

I remember learning my father worked as a steamfitter at the Brooklyn Navy Yard, building warships, because he was blind in his right eye and couldn't be in the Army. He tried. He memorized the chart to pass the eye test. But the first time they handed him a rifle at basic training, and he put it to his left shoulder, he was sent home.

I have a particularly fond memory of May 28, 1944—Memorial Day weekend—when my uncle Irving and my father took me to my first baseball game at Ebbets Field. It was a doubleheader between the Brooklyn Dodgers and Cincinnati Reds. What magic for a boy who turned five years old just twenty-three days before—the bright-green grass and sienna-colored infield dirt, the towering stands, and the fans who were taking a few hours away from the war and everyday pressures to root for the team that instantly became my team for life. Irving and other servicemen in uniform were admitted to the game free. We ate hot dogs and French fries and drank orange Nehi soda. My Dad and Irving explained the game to me and told me the nicknames of the various players: Dixie and Frenchy and years later the likes of Bananas, Goody, Pistol, Shotgun and so many others.

Two months later, Irving was killed at the Battle of the Hedgerows during the liberation of France. Until that day, the telegrams, those awful telegrams from the War Department, had gone to other families in the neighborhood. The word would go out quickly—this one's son, that one's husband wouldn't be coming home. And everyone would rush to help. Now it was our family's turn—my aunt Tillie, my little cousin Linda. The telegram was for them.

Of all the memories of my years on the streets of Brooklyn there's one day and one girl I recall with particular frequency.

It was August 14, 1945, the day Japan surrendered, the day The War ended.

We heard the news the way we heard a lot of news in Brooklyn on hot and humid summer days. From an open window across the courtyard that separated our building from the four-story apartment building next door came a woman's shriek: "The war is over." In an instant, we could hear radios coming on in every apartment. Then there was the crying, the wails of relief, the shouts of joy from the mothers and wives. Now we would be able to live without the specter of those awful telegrams from the War Department: "We regret to inform you ..."

People streamed out of every building. The streets were filled with people crying and smiling at the same time, hugging, clapping each other on the back, and reaching out with extra care for those whose husbands, fathers, brothers, or sons would not be coming home. For them the celebration was muted.

Within hours of that first news bulletin, as if by magic, lumber appeared and was banged together to make a stage at one end of our broad, tree-lined street. Tables covered with red, white, and blue crepe paper lined a traffic lane on each side of the street. Too bad for any cars parked at the curbs; they were blocked for the duration. We were getting ready for the damnedest block party ever and it was happening on blocks all over Brooklyn. The women were cooking enormous amounts of food to be set on the tables that night. People with musical instruments were in the streets playing war songs and Dixieland and Jewish folk songs and Italian songs and jazz.

But what I remember most was our landlord's teenage daughter, Rosie. The echoes of that news hardly had faded when Rosie's voice first filled the courtyard. She was rehearsing the song she planned to sing at the block party that night. Over and over and over again the words echoed through the courtyard: *"It had to be you. It had to be you. I wandered around, and finally found, the somebody who ..."* That night of all nights, she wanted it to be perfect.

Until that day, I had no idea Rosie could sing. Her chief function in the neighborhood, as far as we guys were concerned, was to be ogled by every preteen boy on the block. But that night Rosie was transformed. Made up as we never before had seen her and looking every bit the woman, she stood on that makeshift stage and filled the night with her voice. I stood at the front of the stage and stared in amazement. She lived right upstairs from us, and I never knew.

My mother told me I could stay up as late as I wanted. That never happened before. She said, "Whenever you're tired, just go in the house and go to bed. We'll see you in the morning."

What a wonderful innocence—no hesitation to leave doors unlocked with two younger sisters asleep in the apartment, and no concern about unsupervised young boys on the street after dark. Fireworks lit the sky that night; everyone danced, and sang, and ate. Kegs of beer were tapped and drained, and effigies of Japanese war leaders were hung and burned, and Rosie sang, *"It had to be you. It had to be you. I wandered around, and finally found, the somebody who, could make me be true ..."*

I don't remember getting tired that night or going to bed. My friends and I ran everywhere. We stopped at tables and sampled food from every building. We mimicked phrases we heard from the adults: "Thank God, it's over." Everywhere there was laughter and music and dancing, and tears. The war was over. No more uncles, no more fathers, no more brothers, no more husbands would be dying. There would be no more telegrams. It was a day and a night and a time none of us will ever forget. And every time I hear that song, I remember standing in front of that stage, looking up at Rosie as she sang, "It Had to Be You."

On hot summer days in the old neighborhood in Brooklyn, we often could be found at the soda fountain in the corner drug store, Klackstein's. We would drink Egg Creams or Black and Whites, two treats that still are found only in New York, or at the reunion of transplanted New Yorkers every year at Beverly Hills High School. On rare occasions I'll see one listed on a deli menu in L.A. After the war and until we left for California, my father had his own business delivering seltzer water, Fox's-U-Bet syrups, soda pop, and beer to homes of Jewish families across much of Brooklyn. That meant we always had everything we needed at home to duplicate the treats we drank at Klackstein's.

Soda Fountain Black-and-White

An authentic New York soda fountain Black and White should not be made with measurements. Soda jerks just knew how much of each ingredient to use. So, I guess that makes it the ultimate "to taste" recipe.

> Fox's U-Bet chocolate syrup (use another brand at your own risk)
> milk
> seltzer water, preferably in a syphon bottle
> vanilla ice cream
> whipped cream

Start by pouring about an inch and a half of chocolate syrup into a tapered ice cream soda glass. If that doesn't suit your taste, adjust the amount of syrup next time. Add a couple of inches of milk. With a long soda spoon, mix the chocolate into the milk. The regulation soda jerk way is with an up-and-down motion with the spoon, not round and round. While round and round might do a better job of mixing all the chocolate into the milk, that's not the way it was done by soda jerks in a hurry. Squirt in the seltzer to nearly fill the glass. (There will be a lot of foam at the top, but don't worry.) With the long spoon, give three or four rapid up-and-down motions to the bottom of the glass, and then swirl the spoon through the mixture twice. Drop in a scoop of ice cream. The whole thing should fizz up and spill over the sides of the glass. That's a sign of a job well done. Top the soda with a dollop of whipped cream. Serve with the long spoon to eat the ice cream and a straw for the soda.

Note: Seltzer water should be from an old-fashioned high-pressure syphon seltzer bottle or a fountain-type carbonated cylinder. Plain carbonated water or club soda won't do it. The whipped cream should be real whipped cream, not the kind from an aerosol container. We didn't have whipped cream bullets back then. (You may use a different kind of tall glass if you must, and you may use a whipped cream bullet if you must. But it won't be a 100 percent authentic Brooklyn soda fountain Black and White.)

Soda Fountain Egg Cream

An Egg Cream is the same thing as a Black and White, only it leaves out the ice cream and the whipped cream. No one knows for sure why it's called an Egg Cream, instead of just a chocolate soda, as there is no egg in it. One popular but unproven belief has it that once upon a time it was regulation to stir in a raw egg or egg yolk. If that ever was true, it hasn't happened in generations. And as far as anyone can tell, the drink never did include cream.

Wikipedia has this to say about it: "One theory is that grade A milk was used in its creation, leading to the name 'a chocolate A cream,' which sounded like 'egg' cream. Stanley Auster, the grandson of the beverage's alleged inventor, has been quoted as saying that the origins of the name are lost in time. One commonly accepted belief is that 'egg' is a corruption of the German (also found in Yiddish) word *echt* (genuine or real) and this was a 'good cream.' Food historian Andrew Smith writes: 'During the 1880s, a popular specialty was made with chocolate syrup, cream, and raw eggs mixed into soda water. In poorer neighborhoods, a less expensive version of this treat was created, called the Egg Cream (made without the eggs or cream)'."

CHAPTER THREE
Puppy Love

STOOPS
On "stoops" like these, we would spend hot summer days in Brooklyn playing geography, or just sitting and talking.

POTSY
The girls would play potsy, a variation of hopscotch, while the boys played punch ball in the streets of Brooklyn. Third base could be the fender of a car.

There is no time in the life of a man when a woman can't reduce him to absolute silliness, or worse. A man will idolize a woman, fear a woman, lose his senses in the love of a woman, and lose his sensibility over the loss of a woman. The stupidest things a man will do in his life probably will have something to do with a woman.

Ask a boy of eight or nine or ten what he thinks of girls and he very well might scrunch up his face and say something like, "Girls are yucky."

Why does the teenage boy not ask the cheerleader for a date? Because he's sure she will say "no," and he's worried others will think him silly for daring to ask.

Fortunately, these are afflictions from which I never suffered. I dated the cheerleader and the drum majorette. And, no, I wasn't the quarterback on the football team—or anything else on the football team. I just knew from a very early age that I liked girls.

I was eight years old when I first risked the teasing of the guys in our neighborhood, allowed myself to admit I "liked" a girl, and let myself do something about it.

I had seen what happened when my friend Stanley made the mistake of letting it be known that he "liked" Frances from down the block. The other kids were merciless: "Stanley and Frances sitting in a tree, k-i-s-s-i-n-g" went the chant that followed him everywhere. Or "Stanley loves Frances" was scrawled in chalk on the sidewalk in front of his apartment building.

With that as a warning, I wasn't completely reckless. Her name was Beth and I kept my attraction a secret, even from her.

Beth and I were in the same third grade class. Before I learned that I liked to be with her and talk with her, I knew she was pretty. Her straight, dark-brown, shoulder-length hair reminded me of some of the actresses I saw in the movies. She was taller than most of the other girls in our class, and when she walked down the street, I thought she looked like royalty. One of my cousins, who knew Beth later in their high school years, told me she grew up to be a striking beauty.

Beth lived in the four-story apartment house on the corner of our long street, right next to the two-story brownstone in which we lived. To get to school she had to walk by our building. I could stand at the glass front door of our building and see her coming. Then I could manage to walk out just as she was passing by—every day. By making it seem to happen by chance I believed we could walk to school together without anyone being the wiser.

As soon as we completed the two-block walk and got inside the school gate, we went our separate ways. I joined my friends to play ball if it wasn't raining or snowing, and she was off to find her friends and play hopscotch, or jump rope, or potsy.

At the end of the school day I would manage to get to the playground gate at the same time Beth did so we could walk home together, usually joined by some of the other kids from the neighborhood. In winter we would buy a Charlotte Russe or a baked sweet potato from a pushcart vendor to eat as we walked. When it was warmer, it might be Italian ices, crushed ice with various flavored syrups in paper cones.

If Beth ever caught on to what I was doing, she never said anything. But she never did anything to avoid our "accidental" meetings either. We were two friends walking to and from school together. I managed to keep that up for a full school year, believing the guys, who lived on the same block and were walking in the same direction on the same street, didn't notice what was going on. No one ever teased me. Maybe they actually *didn't* notice.

Sally came into the picture near the end of our third grade year. She had been in the same class with us all year, but I was so focused on Beth that I didn't really notice her until one spring day, when I was walking with my friend Howard to his apartment to do homework after school. Sally was walking in the same direction. She lived two buildings from Howard, a few blocks from where I lived. I got to know her as the three of us walked and talked. That afternoon we studied together in Howard's apartment. That became a routine till the end of the school year—walk to school with Beth, walk home with Beth some days, walk home with Howard and Sally other days.

That summer, I split my time between Howard's block and my own. Ours was a four-lane street with too much traffic to allow us to play the street games common to Brooklyn in those days. Hit-the-penny and stoop ball worked on the sidewalk. But when it came to stick ball or punch ball the street was just too busy and the courtyard between our buildings was too small.

Howard and Sally lived on a narrow street with parking on both sides. That left hardly enough room for two cars to pass in opposite directions. There wasn't much traffic and the block had lots of kids, including Sally, with her sandy-brown hair and olive skin.

I didn't see much of Beth that summer. I think her family went to the mountains for most of the vacation. But Sally was very present. She and the other girls on her block spent their days playing sidewalk games, while we boys played punch ball in the street with our pink Spaldeens. The fender of the Buick might have been first base, the manhole cover second base, the fire hydrant third base, and a flattened cardboard box was home plate. Or it could be drawn with chalk, like the pitcher's "rubber".

On afternoons when it was too hot to do anything else, we sat on the stoop (Brooklynese for front steps) of Howard's building and played geography. That's the game in which one person says the name of a place. The next person must name a place that starts with the last letter of the previous person's place. When someone is stumped or names a place that has been used before, that person is out. It goes on like that until there is only one person left. Sally, Howard and I could keep at it for hours. Usually we were the last ones left in the game; we could go on until we had to quit for supper. I was spending time with Sally, but not in any way that would arouse suspicion. Besides, it was out of the view of the guys on my block.

When school started in September, I resumed my morning and afternoon "liaisons" with Beth. A couple of times each week I would go to Howard's to do homework after school, and Sally might join us.

Part way into our fourth grade year, Carol and her twin brother, Gary, moved into the neighborhood. Carol joined Howard, Beth, Sally and me in the rapid advance section of the school. Gary was in the regular section. He was a good athlete and we all wanted him on our team when we would choose up sides, no matter what we were playing, but scholastically he was a beat behind his twin sister. In class I couldn't keep my eyes off Carol. She had these two crater-size dimples, blue eyes that never stopped smiling, and a sprinkling of freckles. If Beth was the prettiest girl in our grade, Carol was the cutest.

Most Saturday mornings a group of us guys would walk to the end of our block, cross the street, and walk under the elevated train tracks to the Sutter Theater for a double-feature movie plus cartoons and a newsreel. Gary complained that his parents made him take Carol with him most of the time. That was just fine with me. I arrived at the theater each week with yet another plan for how I could spend time with a girl I "liked" without anyone catching on. Even at that young age, the male capacity for self-deception is limitless when it comes to females.

While the rest of the gang went to their seats, I would stop at the snack bar or restroom, secure in the knowledge that the other guys would try to avoid sitting next to Carol. That meant there almost always was an empty seat available beside her. That was my seat. There was no other choice. Why would anyone suspect anything? If she happened to be on an aisle I would just ask everyone to "move down a seat" to make room for me so I didn't have to climb over them.

It worked that way every week. I would sit next to her and we would talk before and between movies. I would share my Good & Plenty candy with her. She was the only girl in the group and I was the only boy who paid her any attention.

What an exciting intrigue all this was—scheming ways to spend time with each of the three girls and trying to keep it secret. I did it so well that I doubt any of the girls knew I "liked" her, let alone knew anything about how I felt toward the other two—or would care if they did know.

Our family left Brooklyn a few months after my tenth birthday. I didn't want to go. There were my friends, there was my position as one of the better students in my grade, there was the Brooklyn Dodgers, and there were the three girls. But my parents were fed up with the New York winters. My Dad had slipped on the ice while carrying a case of seltzer bottles after a snowstorm the previous December. He cracked his kneecap and was still in the hospital when he announced his intention to leave the city where he was born and had lived his entire life. The plan was for us to try it in California for a year. If we didn't like it, we would move back east.

I sent picture postcards to each of the three girls from each stop as we traveled west on legendary Route 66 in our grey Pontiac Silver Cloud. I don't remember the exact words

I wrote. But I think it was some pretty hot stuff for a ten-year-old. I hadn't watched all those movie musicals and romantic comedies for nothing. I know I told each of the girls I missed her and wished I didn't have to leave. The messages in the three postcards were identical. How creative do you think a lovesick ten-year-old can be? I was homesick every mile of the way and the three girls were the embodiment of everything I missed.

Years later, while relating this story to a friend, I realized the danger that might have been waiting for me if we didn't like California. Three girls had a collection of written declarations of how I felt about them. If they compared notes, they might be waiting to kill me. And then there was Gary, Carol's twin brother. How much did he know and what did he share with the other guys? Probably everything. In the end it didn't matter. After trying L.A. for a year, we decided to stay. You see, there was this girl in my fifth grade class in the Silver Lake area of Los Angeles.

It was strange at first, living in L.A. We didn't need to bundle up against the cold in winter. We could play baseball and football and basketball outdoors all year on ground that never was frozen or covered with snow. If we wanted to see snow, we could drive ninety minutes east to the mountains of San Bernardino County. On a lark one day, our family set out on that drive early in the morning and then went to the beach later in the afternoon. That really amused my Dad.

In time I came to love L.A. I wouldn't want to live anywhere else. I became one of those Angelenos who reaches for a jacket when the temperature drops below seventy and jokes that the best part of winter is watching it on TV from Los Angeles.

But part of me never left Brooklyn. Even after all these years, every time I visit New York I feel like I'm home. There's nothing like stepping out of your hotel into a New York evening or leaving a Manhattan theater at 11 p.m. to find the streets packed with people, or strolling on the boardwalk at Coney Island with a million people on a holiday weekend. To live in Los Angeles and visit New York regularly—that's about as much as I can ask.

I went back to my old neighborhood in Brooklyn a few times through the years. From the sidewalk, I looked at the old apartment house, which now has been converted to condos. I walked the streets where Beth and I walked to school. Klackstein's Drug Store, Abie's Grocery Store, Harry's Butcher Shop ... they're all gone. The neighborhood isn't the same Jewish and Italian mix it was back then. Caribbean music came from many of the shops the last time I visited. I went to look at the street where Howard and I and the other guys played punch ball and where we sat with Sally and played geography. I walked under the elevated train tracks to the Sutter Theater, where Carol and I shared boxes of Good & Plenty. It was closed and boarded up.

Among the things I recall fondly from those days on the streets of Brooklyn are the pushcart vendors and the pickling plant halfway between home and school. Pushcart peddlers sold all sorts of foodstuffs over the years. In winter it would be Charlotte Russes, or roasted chestnuts, or baked sweet potatoes. In warmer weather it was more likely to be ice cream or flavored Italian ices. Often, we would stop at the pickling plant on the way home from school. They made kosher dill pickles, pickled tomatoes, and sauerkraut. There were penny pickles, two-cent pickles and nickel pickles big enough to share with a friend.

Here are my recipes for two favorites from the old neighborhood.

Pushcart Charlotte Russe

The "cups" in which vendors sold the Charlotte Russe were round cardboard containers with a bottom that slid up to push the whipped cream to the top as you ate. You are not likely to have such a cup, so we'll do this differently.

> 1 large, flat shortcake (or packaged individual shortcakes)
> 1 pint heavy (whipping) cream
> 1/4 cup sugar
> 2 teaspoons vanilla extract
> chocolate sprinkles (optional)

Trim the shortcakes to fit the bottoms of dessert cups. Put the cream and sugar in a deep mixing bowl. Beat it until it turns to whipped cream. Fold in the vanilla extract to incorporate thoroughly. Spoon the whipped cream over the shortcake in the dessert cups. Keep refrigerated until it's time to serve. Serve the sprinkles in a separate bowl as an optional topping.

This will make enough whipped cream for about eight tall desserts.

ADULT VERSION
The adult version is my own adaptation. Mix 1/4 cup of Grand Marnier in with the whipping cream and drip about a teaspoon of Grand Marnier over each piece of shortcake before adding the whipped cream.

Kosher Dill Pickles

This is the recipe my mother wrote for me on a 3" x 5" card. It probably dates back more than 130 years to her mother in Romania.

> 4 pounds of unwaxed pickling cucumbers (3 to 4 inches long)
> 1/2 cup coarse koshering salt
> 1 head garlic, halved horizontally (leave the paper on)
> 1 teaspoon whole black peppercorns
> 1/2 teaspoon red pepper flakes
> 1/4 package fresh dill (about 6 or 7 full sprigs)
> cool tap water

Scrub the cucumbers to remove any sand and grit, but don't break the skins. Trim any stems from the ends of the cucumbers. Stand the cucumbers, thick end down, in a 1-gallon glass jar. (You should get three layers of cucumbers. If there are any extras, lay them on top.) Pour the salt over the cucumbers. Break apart the halved garlic cloves and drop them into the jar. Drop the black peppercorns and red pepper flakes into the jar. Push the dill stalks into the jar between the cucumbers. Fill the jar with cold tap water to cover the cucumbers. Rotate the jar sharply to distribute the salt and other ingredients.

If any cucumbers float to the top, place a glass filled with water in the mouth of jar to hold them down. Drape a lightweight cloth over the top of the jar to cover the mouth. Place the jar on a counter and let it stand at room temperature four to six days or until the cucumbers take on the dark green color of dill pickles. After the second day, rotate the jar back and forth sharply to redistribute the water and other ingredients. When the pickles are done, remove them from the jar. Pour the liquid through a strainer to remove the solids. Put the pickles into smaller jars, pour in the strained pickling liquid, cover the jars, and refrigerate.

Note: In selecting cucumbers, buy only ones that are firm. Soft ones have of a tendency to hollow out in the center during the pickling process. That may happen to some of the pickles anyway, but firm ones are less likely to suffer this problem. Don't worry, though. Even the hollowed ones will be crunchy and taste wonderful.

CHAPTER FOUR
California, Here I Am

TAMALES
She was the first Mexican person I ever knew and I tasted Mexican food for the first time with her family at their home.

HAPPY BIRTHDAY
What a fuss her family made when they learned my birthday is on the Mexican holiday of Cinco de Mayo. They bought a birthday piñata just for me.

The first time I saw Yolanda Quintero she was sitting on a bench in the shade near the sun-drenched concrete playground at the elementary school we attended near downtown Los Angeles. She was reading a book.

It was morning recess, my first day at a new school a continent away from the friends and familiar life I left behind in Brooklyn. I showed up that morning wearing a dress shirt and tie with slacks, just what I wore to school on the other coast. All the other boys were wearing blue jeans, T-shirts and sneakers. It was going to be a challenge to fit into this new place.

I stood and watched the other kids play dodge ball or kick ball or tether ball, games I never heard of in Brooklyn. I thought they were silly games. The midmorning, early September temperature already had climbed to over eighty degrees. So I strolled over to the shade at the cream-colored, picnic-style lunch tables.

Yolanda was sitting at one of those tables. I sat on the bench on the opposite side at the other end of the table. She glanced up from her book and I said "hello." I told her my name and she told me hers. I loved her Mexican accent, and she seemed to understand my Brooklyn accent. I told her I was from New York and new at the school. I looked into her brown eyes as we spoke. She had the longest eyelashes I ever had seen, brown hair that was lightened by the sun, olive skin, and a sweet smile. I remember she looked so *soft*. When recess ended, I said I would see her at lunchtime. She said, "okay."

We ate lunch together that day for the first time, just the two of us, apart from the other kids. I told her about New York and my life there, leaving out the part about Beth, Sally and Carol. I learned she came to Los Angeles from Mexico two years earlier and lived across the street from the school with her mother, father and two older brothers, who attended a nearby junior high school.

At lunch the next day, I asked if she would like to meet at the neighborhood movie theater Saturday. She said she would ask her parents. The following day she told me her parents wanted to know who she was going with, so I went to her house after school and met her mother. Mrs. Quintero was tall and beautiful. I thought she could have been a movie star. She served us lemonade and cookies. She asked about my family, where we lived, why we left New York, all with a heavy and challenging Mexican accent.

That Saturday, I had my first real date—sort of. I left my bike at Yolanda's house and we walked to the theater. We each paid our own admission; I bought the candy. I told my parents I was going to the movies with a friend. I didn't mention that the friend was a girl. At Back to School Night a couple of weeks later, our teacher told Mom and Dad how Yolanda and I had become inseparable.

We were not in the same grade at the start of the school year. But two weeks into the semester I was moved up a grade because my New York schooling had me far ahead of kids the same age in L.A. It didn't put much of a dent in the gap, which didn't actually close until I reached college. I was ten years old when I walked into my new classroom—Yolanda's class. She was twelve. She had been held back a grade level because of language issues when her family emigrated from Mexico. That made her the oldest kid in the class; I was the youngest.

Yolanda Quintero was the first Mexican person I ever met. She was the only Mexican kid in the school; I was the only Jewish kid. I think everyone else was blonde.

In the waning days of summer vacation, soon after we moved into the neighborhood, I met a boy named Don. He was a year older than I was and lived near us in the hills of the Silver Lake neighborhood of Los Angeles. As we bicycled home from school together on the first day of classes, I asked him, "Tell me about Yolanda," whom I had just met that day.

"She's Mexican," he answered.

How prophetic. Here was this lovely girl who had been in the same class with him for more than a year. Yet all he knew about her was, "She's Mexican." He didn't even make some juvenile remark about her figure, which was far more developed than that of any other girl in the school. I was at the school just one day and I knew more about her than he did.

Years later, white California would have a great deal of trouble getting comfortable with a burgeoning Latino population. That problem still plagues people in many parts of the U.S. and causes them to want to build fences "to keep *them* out." Perhaps it is because they know nothing more about their Latino neighbors than Don knew about Yolanda: "They're Mexican." If they took the time to know their neighbors the way I got to know the Quintero family we'd all be the better for it.

In our Brooklyn neighborhood, if you weren't Jewish you most likely would have been Italian. The only difference was where you went to pray and on what day. Otherwise, it came down to family, food, music, and how well you could play baseball. It was no surprise, then, that when I met Yolanda's family, I fit right in. The Mexican culture that filled their home was very much the same as what I knew in my old Brooklyn neighborhood—always family, food, and music. I ate Mexican food for the first time at a family gathering in their backyard.

The rest of that school year, I spent most recesses and

lunchtimes with Yolanda, usually sitting in the shade talking, reading, or doing our homework together. Yolanda was the reason I woke up wanting to go to school each morning. My lessons were boring. Except for California History, I had taken it all two or three years earlier in Brooklyn. We were doing simple arithmetic; I got an A in beginning algebra the year before.

It shouldn't have bothered any of the other boys in our class that Yolanda and I were spending so much time together. They had ignored her for two years. Maybe it was because they were inching toward puberty and didn't know what to do about it; maybe it was because they didn't understand the funny way I talked or the New York attitude I brought with me; maybe it was the way Yolanda was blossoming into a lovely teenager; or maybe it was the way Yolanda and I made no attempt to conceal our friendship—but it bothered a few of the guys enough that they tried to pick a fight with me. I just walked away.

Yolanda and I continued to meet at the movie theater two or three Saturdays each month. Some afternoons I would go to her house after school and we would do homework together before I bicycled home.

In spring we had to learn some songs for a celebration of the Mexican holiday of Cinco de Mayo. Of course, Yolanda already knew those songs. She became my personal tutor. Mexican songs with a Brooklyn accent ... it must have been something to hear. We laughed a lot, and I celebrated the holiday at the Quintero home. Cinco de Mayo (the Fifth of May) also happens to be my birthday. I had two birthday parties that year—one with my family and one at the Quintero home. They sang "Happy Birthday" to me in Spanish and had a birthday piñata for me. A month later, school ended. Two months after that we moved to another part of Los Angeles and I never saw Yolanda again. But knowing her made me stop wanting to go back to Brooklyn. In the brief span of the one school year I knew them, the Quintero family gave me all I would need to appreciate life in Los Angeles as the Mexican population grew in the decades that followed.

I never heard of a taco or an enchilada in New York. At Yolanda's house, with her parents, brothers, and family friends, I tasted these and just about every other kind of Mexican food. That's where I ate *mole* for the first time, and it remains a favorite all these years later. Enchiladas, taquitos, carne asada, tamales ... it was all homemade and wonderful. I even learned to use Mrs. Quintero's tortilla press.

The recipes that follow are my own creations for Mexican dishes. Often, when I prepare them, I see Yolanda's mother smiling and hear her saying, as she did then, "You are Mexican in your soul."

You'll notice that I leave out the lard and cut back on the salt in these recipes. This is at the behest of my cardiologist, who told me, after my quadruple coronary bypass, that I should stay away from Mexican restaurants.

Chili con Carne

Chili is a spice—actually a variety of peppers that are used as spice, often dried and powdered. It also is used as the name of a Mexican food. Chili at the Quintero home did not include beans. Neither does authentic chili in Mexico, where chili is a meat dish with a chili sauce. Carne is the Spanish word for meat and con means with. All of this leads me to wonder about the Americanized name for this dish: Chili con Carne. Since chili is a meat dish, doesn't that mean meat with meat?(And yes, I know better.)

> 2 tablespoons extra-virgin olive oil
> 1/2 pound lean ground beef
> 1 (15-ounce) can no-salt-added pinto beans
> 1 (7-ounce) can chopped green chilis (mild or hot to taste)
> 1/4 teaspoon ground chili powder, more or less to taste
> 1 teaspoon ground cumin
> 1/2 teaspoon dried oregano
> 1 medium tomato, coarsely chopped
> salt to taste
> 4 tortillas (flour or corn, as per your taste)
> 1/2 cup onion, coarsely chopped

Heat the oil in a large frying pan. Add the ground beef and break it apart with a wooden spoon. Keep breaking it apart and stirring it until almost all the pink is gone. Add the beans, including the liquid from the can. Stir well with the beef. Stir in the green chilis. Add the chili powder, cumin, and oregano and stir well. Add the tomato and stir well.

Cover and cook at a slow boil for 15 minutes. Add salt to taste. Heat the tortillas in a warm frying pan and cover on a plate to keep them warm.

Serve the chili in a bowl topped with 1/4 cup of chopped onion. Serve the tortillas on the side.

Serves two.

Beef Tacos

> 4 tablespoons vegetable oil, divided
> 1 large onion, halved and sliced, divided
> 2 pounds blade-cut beef chuck, cut in chunks with most of the fat trimmed
>
> 1 cup water
> 1/4 cup chopped onion
> 1 garlic clove, chopped
> 1 (7-ounce) can green chili salsa
> 1 (4-ounce) can diced green chilis
> 1/2 teaspoon salt
> 1 cup chopped fresh cilantro
> 8 tortillas (flour or corn)
> 3 cups shredded lettuce
> 2 large tomatoes, chopped
> 3 cups each shredded cheddar and Jack cheese
> 1 (8-ounce) container sour cream

Heat 2 tablespoons of oil in a large frying pan. Sauté the sliced onions until they begin to brown. Add the beef and toss it to sear on all sides. Add the water. Turn the heat to low. Cover and stew the beef and onions until all the liquid is gone, stirring occasionally. The onions should be well browned and the meat should pull apart easily. Add more water and stew longer if necessary. Remove the beef to a plate and shred it either by hand or using two forks. In a medium skillet, heat the remaining oil. Add the chopped onion and garlic. Sauté until the onion is soft but not browned. Mix in the salsa, chilis, salt, and the stewed beef and onions. Simmer, uncovered, 10 minutes or until heated through. Transfer to a serving bowl and stir in the cilantro.

Warm the tortillas and stack them on a plate for serving. Cover them with a cloth napkin to keep in the warmth. Serve the lettuce, tomatoes, cheeses and sour cream in serving bowls so each person can take as much or as little as they want.

Makes enough for eight to ten tacos

Chicken Tacos

> 2 chicken thighs (skinless and boneless)
> 1 teaspoon ground cumin
> 1/4 teaspoon ground chili powder (or to taste)
> 2 tablespoons extra-virgin olive oil plus 1 teaspoon
> 4 tortillas (flour or corn)
> 1/2 cup diced white onion
> 1/2 cup taco sauce (or more to taste)
> 1/2 teaspoon sriracha sauce (or to taste)

Slice the chicken into quarter-inch-wide strips. Slice the strips into quarter-inch pieces. Put 1 teaspoon of olive oil in a glass bowl. Add the chicken and toss to coat. Sprinkle the chicken with the cumin and chili powder, and toss to distribute evenly.

Heat the rest of the oil over medium-high heat in a wide frying pan. Add the chicken and toss. Fry the chicken until it loses its raw color. Raise the heat to medium-high. Fry the chicken until well browned, stirring frequently to prevent burning.

Heat the tortillas in a separate frying pan. Put two tortillas on each of two plates. Spoon the chicken across the center of each tortilla. Distribute the onions on top of the chicken. Spoon the taco sauce on top of the onions. Add the sriracha sauce on top of the taco sauce.

Serve with refried beans.

Serves two.

Cheese Enchiladas

> 1 cup sour cream
> 1 1/2 cups small-curd cottage cheese
> 1 cup sliced green onions
> 1 (7-ounce) can diced green chilis
> 12 tortillas (flour or corn)
> canola oil
> 9 ounces Jack cheese, shredded, divided
> 1 avocado, sliced
> enchilada sauce (see following)

Combine the sour cream, cottage cheese, green onions and chilies and set aside. Heat a wide frying pan—preferably nonstick—and warm the tortillas in the pan, turning once. As the tortillas are ready, remove each onto a plate. Spoon 1/4 cup of the sour cream mixture across the center of each tortilla. Sprinkle Jack cheese on each tortilla. (Set aside about 1/2 cup of the Jack cheese for topping.) Roll the tortillas and place seam side down in a 9" x 13" baking dish that has been lightly coated with oil. Spoon the enchilada sauce over the filled tortillas. Bake at 350 degrees 15 minutes or until heated through. Just before serving, top with avocado slices and sprinkle with the remaining Jack cheese. Place under the broiler for a few seconds to melt the cheese.

Enchilada Sauce

> 1 (15-ounce) can tomato sauce
> 1/2 cup water
> 2 1/2 teaspoons chili powder
> 1 teaspoon salt
> 1/2 teaspoon garlic powder
> 1/4 teaspoon ground cumin
> Dash hot pepper sauce

Combine all ingredients in a saucepan and simmer 20 minutes.

Chicken Enchiladas

> 6 tablespoons vegetable oil, divided
> 1/3 cup diced onion
> 2 1/2 tablespoons flour, divided
> 1 (8-ounce) can tomato sauce
> 1/2 teaspoon chili powder
> 1/4 teaspoon dried crushed oregano
> 1/4 teaspoon garlic powder
> 1/2 teaspoon salt
> 2 cups diced cooked chicken (dark meat preferred)
> 1 cup sour cream
> 12 tortillas (flour or corn)
> 1 cup half-and-half
> 1/2 cup chicken broth
> 1 cup shredded Jack or sharp cheddar cheese

Heat 3 tablespoons of oil in a medium saucepan. Add the onions and sauté 4 minutes. Add 1 tablespoon flour and cook, stirring until the flour is browned. Add the tomato sauce, chili powder, oregano, garlic powder, and salt; stir to incorporate with the flour. Simmer, uncovered, 10 minutes. Add the chicken and sour cream and mix well. Set aside.

Heat the remaining oil in a large skillet. Heat a separate wide frying pan—preferably non-stick—and warm the tortillas in the pan, turning once. Combine the half-and-half and broth in a saucepan and heat. Make a paste with the remaining 1 1/2 tablespoons of flour and a small amount of the half-and-half mixture. Stir the paste into the remaining mixture of half-and-half and broth; cook and stir until thickened. Dip the heated tortillas into the cream mixture. Spoon about 1/4 cup of filling onto each tortilla. Roll and place seam side down in a 9" x 13" or equivalent size baking dish that has been lightly coated with oil. Pour the remaining sauce over the enchiladas, and sprinkle with cheese. Bake at 350 degrees 20 minutes, until cheese is melted.

Makes six servings of two enchiladas each

Steak Ranchero

> 1 tablespoon vegetable oil
> 2 pounds round steak, thinly sliced and cut into 2-inch strips
> salt and pepper to taste
> 1 medium onion, sliced
> 1 jalapeño chili, sliced thin, seeds and spines removed
> 1 garlic clove, minced
> 2 medium tomatoes, chopped
> 1/4 teaspoon dried thyme
> 1 (8-ounce) can tomato sauce
> 1 cup beer
> 1 teaspoon Worcestershire sauce
> 1/2 cup sliced mushrooms

Heat the oil in a wide skillet. Brown the steak in the oil about 15 minutes, stirring frequently. Salt and pepper the meat to taste. Add the onion, chilies, garlic, tomatoes and thyme. Cover and cook over medium heat for 15 minutes. Add the tomato sauce, beer, Worcestershire sauce and mushrooms. Simmer, covered, for 45 minutes.

Serve with Spanish rice, refried beans, and flour tortillas, either freshly made or warmed in a preheated (preferably non-stick) frying pan.

Makes eight servings

Shrimp Ranchero

> 1/2 pound medium size shrimp, peeled and cleaned
> 1 tablespoon vegetable oil
> 2 garlic cloves, minced
> 1 onion, chopped
> 1 Anaheim chili, cut in thin 1-inch strips, seeds and spine removed
> 1 medium tomato, chopped
> 4 ounces tomato sauce
> salt and pepper

Slice the shrimp in half lengthwise. Heat the oil in a skillet. Add the garlic, onion and chili and cook until the onion is tender. Add the shrimp, tomatoes, and tomato sauce. Season lightly with salt and pepper. Cover and cook until shrimp is no longer pink, about 5 to 6 minutes.

Serve with fluffy long-grain white rice or Spanish rice.

Serves two.

Guacamole

> 4 large ripe avocados, mashed
> 1/4 cup onion, finely diced
> 2 tablespoons lime juice (or more to taste)
> 1/2 teaspoon sweet paprika
> salt to taste
> Tabasco sauce to taste
> 1/4 teaspoon chili powder (or more to taste)
> 1 medium tomato, chopped (or more to taste)
> 1/3 cup coarsely chopped cilantro
> extra-virgin olive oil, as needed

Mix together the mashed avocados, onion, lime juice, and paprika. Mix in the salt and Tabasco to taste. Mix in chili powder to taste. Stir in the tomatoes and cilantro. For a creamier Guacamole, mix in some olive oil to taste.

Makes about three to four cups of dip.

Spanish Rice

> 1 cup long-grain white rice
> 3 tablespoons butter or olive oil
> 1 medium onion, diced finely
> 1 1/2 cups canned, peeled tomatoes, chopped (juice drained into a measuring cup)
> enough water to bring tomato juice to 2 cups
> 1/4 to 1/2 teaspoon cumin, to taste
> 1/2 teaspoon salt, or to taste

Soak the rice in hot tap water to cover for 15 minutes. Drain and rinse in cool running tap water until the water is clear. Spread the rice on a paper towel or lint-free cloth to dry. Heat the butter or oil in a saucepan. Add the rice and cook, stirring often, until rice is golden. Add the onion, tomatoes, tomato juice, cumin and salt. Cover and simmer over low heat until the juice is evaporated and rice is dry and flaky, about 20 minutes.

Serves four.

CHAPTER FIVE

First Touch

TONY BENNETT'S STAR ON HOLLYWOOD BLVD
I was trapped. It was be cool or be a fool. I had to dance, even though I didn't know how. Fortunately, it was a slow dance.

Words and music ... a song ... a memory ...
Not many things can define the depth of passion possible between two people so clearly and quickly as a tune that lingers through the years and recalls moments of discovery, tenderness, and sometimes loss.

There's the song that identifies the most passionate romance of your life—the person who touched you the most deeply when he or she entered your life, the person who hurt you most by leaving.

Remember the "enchanted evening" when you first saw him "across a crowded room," or when she went away and in your head you heard the words, "I'll be seeing you."

What is the sexiest song you ever heard?

Cole Porter's classic "Night and day, you are the one ..."? Or maybe the poetry of his "Begin the Beguine"?

Barbra Streisand's "He Touched Me" or "I've Never Been a Woman Before"?

What about Charles Aznavour's "We can never know how love takes over every heart ..." or "After Loving You," "She," or "I Live for You"?

Ask a thousand people and you'll get two thousand answers. Maybe more. It all comes down to the moment and the memories.

My personal sentimental choice is Tony Bennett singing "Because of You". It was the song that was playing on a chilly

January night in 1954, when I danced with a girl for the first time and learned what it's like to hold a girl in my arms and feel the softness of her and know the scent of her.

Dancing back then was different than it is now. People touched each other, put their arms around each other and danced close together. Even while they danced to Bill Haley and the Comets in the early days of rock 'n roll, they held hands much of the time.

I stayed away from school dances throughout three years in junior high school. So did most of my friends. Thirteen-year-old boys talked a good game when it came to girls. But dancing meant asking and touching, and those were things for which most guys our age were not ready. Asking meant risking rejection; touching was something we were beginning to want desperately but were not necessarily sure how to do. Besides, certain things were happening in our denims at inopportune times, and touching to dance might bring on one of those times. Then what would we do?

Then came the dance honoring our graduating class—kind of a prom without all the expense and hoopla that accompanies such events today. My friends and I talked it over and decided to give it a try.

The biggest hurdle for me was that I didn't know how to dance. But this was the last dance of my last semester in junior high school. Maybe I could fake my way through the evening without actually having to dance.

That fantasy was blown apart by something called a Sadie Hawkins dance, named after the comic book character who aggressively pursued Li'l Abner. It meant it was the girls' turn to ask the boys to dance.

In my pressed white peggers (denims), powder-blue sport shirt with Elvis-like sparkling silver threads and my blue suede shoes, I was standing off to the side of the gym, talking with some friends and paying no attention to the dance floor. I didn't notice Linda as she approached, although I'm not sure what I would have done if I had seen her coming.

I was familiar with the blueness of her eyes, the way her medium-brown hair hung just to the base of her neck, and the tiny brown birthmark at the corner of her mouth. I saw them every day across the aisle in American history class. But in all the time I had known her, I don't think we exchanged fifty words. When we did talk, it was about school assignments.

Linda could have asked any one of us to dance, but to the relief of every other boy in the group, she asked me. The only dancing I had done before that moment was the minuet in a play about George Washington in fourth grade and square dancing, which I hated, in gym class.

What a challenge—be cool or be a fool. "No" was not an option. Fortunately, it was a slow dance. It would involve touching and Linda was one of the girls in our class many of the guys would like to have touched. I was trapped; I said "okay," and we walked a few steps to the dance floor in stocking feet so as not to ruin the gym floor.

I assumed the position and tried to act as if I were an old hand at this dancing business. The student band was on a break, so a recording of Tony Bennett singing "Because of You" was cued up on the hi-fidelity record player. It was a good song to start with because I didn't have to do much—just shuffle my feet in approximate time with the music and not lift them high enough to step on her. It would have been a lot easier if not for the distraction of feeling things pressed against me that I'd never felt before. Then Linda said something; I answered and soon we were talking and I was dancing without thinking about every step, or about her anatomy.

I danced a few more times that night—always with Linda. Once I even did the asking. It was the polite thing to do.

As the evening was ending, Linda asked if I wanted to walk home with her and a few other kids. I lived about a mile from the school and by the time we got to my street everyone else had peeled off to their homes except Linda and me. Her house was a few blocks passed mine, so I walked her home. At her front door, she turned and kissed me lightly on the cheek and said good night. I was caught so off guard that she opened the door and vanished into the house before I could react—which probably was a good thing, because I wouldn't have had any idea what to do or say. I mumbled, "Good night" to the closed door and hurried home.

The next Monday at school, some of the guys teased me and asked whether Linda wore falsies. I don't know what made them think I would know.

It would be romantic if I could say that night was the start of something lasting. But it wasn't. We moved on to high school, where Linda and I had different groups of friends. We didn't see each other much outside of the few classes we had together. If we passed in the hall we would exchange greetings and a smile. On a few occasions, when we were at the same party, we would spend some time talking. But we never dated and we never touched again. Still, every time I hear Tony Bennett sing "Because of You" I think of Linda—the first girl I ever held in my arms.

I heard someone say a long time ago, "Dancing is a prelude to seduction." It may have been true of the kind of dancing we used to do. Dancing in the fifties meant moving horizontally around and across the floor. Today, dancers mostly bounce up and down. They dance with such vigor that I'm not sure how they have the energy for seduction or anything else when they're through. I haven't danced much in my life. It's not something I enjoy, probably because I'm not very good at it.

Or am I not very good because I never learned to do it well enough to enjoy it?

Linda and I lived in a suburb of Los Angeles at the edge of the San Fernando Valley. The image of backyard swimming pools and barbecues still lingers at the mention of The Valley, even though it now has grown to where it would be the fifth-largest city in the nation were it to split off from Los Angeles. So, with a smile in my heart for Linda, here are a few barbecue recipes I developed long after the night we touched.

Barbecue Ribs (spare, baby back, or St. Louis), indoors or out

> 1 whole rack of ribs
> Larry's original barbecue sauce (see following)
> granulated garlic (if cooking on an outdoor grill)

Trim any large pieces of fat from the ribs. Cut the rack into pieces of two or three larger ribs, or three or four smaller ribs. Place the ribs in a large pot and cover with cold tap water. Bring to a boil and boil slowly for 20 minutes. Remove the ribs and discard the water.

If making the ribs indoors, put them into a roasting pan and brush on both sides with the barbeque sauce. Cover and roast at 350 degrees for 40 minutes. For cooking outdoors on a grill, after the ribs have been boiled, sprinkle them with granulated garlic and cook over hot coals, turning frequently. When ribs are almost done, brush on barbecue sauce and cook over the coals until done.

This recipe would serve two, with sides of beans, corn, and/or salad. I have an insatiable appetite for ribs; I usually want a full rack for myself and skip the distraction of the sides.

Larry's Original Barbecue Sauce

> 3 tablespoons vegetable oil
> 1 small onion, chopped
> 1 clove of garlic, chopped
> 4 tablespoons tomato ketchup
> 3 tablespoons soy sauce
> 1 tablespoon Worcestershire sauce
> several drops Tabasco sauce (to taste)
> 1/2 tablespoon white vinegar
> 1 tablespoon honey
> 1 teaspoon each chili powder and cumin
> 1/2 teaspoon each cayenne, dry mustard, powdered ginger, crushed dried thyme and marjoram

Heat the oil in a frying pan. Sauté the onion until lightly browned. Add the garlic and sauté about three minutes. Remove the onion and garlic to a bowl. Add all the other ingredients to the pan. Mix together thoroughly and heat through. Add the onion and garlic to the mixture, stir and let sit several hours at room temperature so flavors can blend. Refrigerate if you are not going to use the sauce immediately.

Let the sauce return to room temperature before using. Brush the sauce on ribs, a tri-tip roast, or chicken before cooking. Baste again with sauce about 15 minutes before the cooking is finished. You may also wish to heat the sauce and serve it in a gravy boat for those who might like a heavier dose with their ribs, beef, or chicken.

Makes enough for one rack of ribs, a tri-tip roast, or a chicken.

Stovetop Barbecue Chicken

> 1 whole fryer chicken, 3 1/2 to 4 1/2 pounds*
> 2 tablespoons vegetable oil
> 1/3 cup soy sauce
> 1/3 cup apple juice concentrate
> 1/2 cup water
> 1 tablespoon tomato ketchup
> 2 tablespoons maple syrup
> 3/4 teaspoon Sriracha sauce or red pepper flakes
> 1 garlic clove, crushed
> 1 green onion, sliced

Cut the chicken into parts, removing any large lumps of fat. Heat the oil in a frying pan. Brown the chicken in the oil. Pour off the oil from the pan. Mix together the soy sauce, apple juice, water, ketchup, maple syrup, Sriracha sauce or pepper flakes, garlic and onion. Pour the mixture over the chicken. Cover and simmer 35 to 40 minutes.

For a lower-fat version of this, remove the skin from the chicken. Coat the chicken lightly with oil. Broil the chicken parts about 10 minutes on each side instead of browning it in a frying pan. Transfer the chicken parts to a frying pan and proceed with the rest of the recipe.

Serves four.

I often use chicken parts—thighs preferred—instead of a whole chicken.

Barbecue Style Beans

> 2 tablespoons extra-virgin olive oil
> 1 small brown onion, coarsely chopped
> 2 garlic cloves, chopped
> 1 large tomato, diced and seeded
> 1 3-ounce can tomato paste
> 1 tablespoon maple syrup
> 1 tablespoon white vinegar
> 1 tablespoon Worcestershire sauce
> 1 teaspoon dry hot mustard
> 1/2 teaspoon cayenne pepper
> 1 (4-ounce) can fire-roasted diced green chilis
> several twists fresh ground black pepper
> 1 (15-ounce) can no-salt-added pinto beans

Warm the olive oil in a small frying pan. Add the onion and sauté until soft. Add the next ten ingredients. Simmer about 20 minutes. Put the beans and their liquid into the pan with the sauce. Return to a simmer and let simmer until beans are heated—about 5 minutes.

To serve, remove the beans from the sauce with a slotted spoon. Then spoon a little sauce over the beans to taste. You won't want the beans swimming in sauce, but you'll want enough sauce to keep the beans moist. You can freeze the leftover sauce.

Southwest Black Beans and Chicken

For the Chicken
2 tablespoons olive oil
1 teaspoon ground cumin
1 teaspoon chili powder
1 teaspoon granulated garlic
1 teaspoon dried oregano
2 large chicken thighs, skinless and boneless

For the Beans
1 (15-ounce) can of no-salt-added black beans (retain the liquid)
1/2 teaspoon Creole or Santa Fe spice mixture
2 teaspoons ground cumin
1 teaspoon salt
1/2 cup coarsely diced onion

Mix together the olive oil, cumin, chili powder, garlic, and oregano. Coat both sides of the chicken with the mixture. Let the chicken marinate in the mixture for 15 minutes at room temperature; turn it over and marinate another 15 minutes.

Make sure the chicken has a good coating of the oil and spices. Place the chicken on a rack and broil for 10 minutes at medium broil four inches from the heat source. Turn the chicken and broil another 10 minutes.

Heat the black beans in a saucepan. When the liquid starts to boil, mash the beans with a potato ricer. Add the spices and salt.

Put 1/4 cup of diced onions at the bottom of each of two bowls. Spoon the beans over the onions. Mix the beans and onions together. Put a chicken thigh on top of the beans in each bowl.

Serves two.

CHAPTER SIX

The Christian Missionary and the Kid from Brooklyn

HIGH SCHOOL GRADUATION
I was seventeen years old when this high school graduation photo was snapped in 1956.

Twenty-four hours earlier, Elizabeth Blackstone was a happy memory from my high school days. Now, I was looking into her still-clear, 101-year-old eyes at a table in a restaurant across the street from Warner Brothers Studios in Burbank, California.

It was the afternoon before the dinner to celebrate the fiftieth anniversary of my high school graduation. I hadn't seen Mrs. Blackstone since graduation day in 1957, and it was only by a happy accident that I wound up at that luncheon table with that very memorable teacher.

I had decided to boycott the reunion dinner because it was being held at a local country club that discriminated against women in its membership policies. Women couldn't be full equity members; six days a week they were relegated to off-peak golf starting times unless they were playing in the company of a male member.

When I learned, a year before, that the reunion committee planned to use the country club for the dinner party, I asked that they move the event and I explained my reason. They told me they already had posted a $1,000 deposit. I assured them the club would return the deposit rather than risk any publicity regarding their membership practices. I offered to refund the $1,000 myself if the club wouldn't. The committee decided to keep the event at the club.

To prove I was boycotting the country club and not my

former classmates, I stopped in at a cocktail party at a local hotel the night before the scheduled dinner. At the cocktail party someone asked which teacher had the greatest impact on me in high school. Without hesitation, I answered, "Elizabeth Blackstone."

"Really," one of the women said, and she called for one of the other women to join the conversation. They told me a small group of former students would be having lunch with Mrs. Blackstone the next day.

"She's still alive?" I gasped. "How can I get in on that lunch?"

Her daughter had put a limit of eight people at the lunch and the table already was booked full. But one of the men, my old friend Wally, had said he might not be able to make it. I told them I would be happy to be on standby, "Call me if Wally can't make it."

I dressed the next morning as I would want to be dressed for lunch with Elizabeth Blackstone at a nice restaurant: sports coat and tie over nicely pressed trousers. I got the call in my office at 11 a.m. "Wally can't make it." An hour later, we were sitting at a table at the Smoke House restaurant: Elizabeth Blackstone, her daughter, five former members of the Campus Christian Club, and me.

Elizabeth Blackstone understood me better than any other teacher in my three years of high school. She put up with more nonsense from me than any teacher should have.

It would be difficult to construct a more unlikely pairing. She and her husband had been Christian missionaries in China for twenty-three years. They fled just weeks before the Communist takeover in 1949. That staid, white-haired, fifty-one-year-old, conservative woman was the faculty advisor to the Campus Christian Club. I was a Jewish teenage street kid from Brooklyn transplanted to Southern California.

We tested each other and challenged each other through my final semester of high school. We laughed together—a lot—and we respected each other. I learned to use chopsticks at a dinner in her home.

By the time I arrived in Mrs. Blackstone's Senior Problems class for my last semester of high school, I had long since lost all interest in academics. High school was a place where I could coordinate my social life. My journalism classes were the only ones that mattered to me. In Brooklyn, I had been in the rapid-advance section at school. That meant you moved through the academic program as rapidly as you could. Had we stayed in Brooklyn I would have finished high school at fourteen. Schools in L.A. had no way to hold the interest of someone like that.

The Senior Problems class was a hodgepodge of things the school district thought we needed to know but hadn't been taught in any other class through eleven and a half years of schooling. We learned how to maintain a checking account and balance a checkbook. We learned how to read a utility bill. We learned about different forms of local government and what they meant to our lives. There also was a hash of other one or two-week study units that were mostly inane and highly forgettable.

None of that mattered as we sat in that restaurant fifty years later. At 101, Mrs. Blackstone was alert and keenly alive. She smiled and laughed and talked with six former students who had gathered to tell her how much she meant to us. From her daughter we learned Mrs. Blackstone still played piano by ear, and friends and relatives called her Betty. After fifty years of her being Elizabeth Blackstone in my memory, Betty Blackstone didn't seem right.

As the years rolled by after high school, my appreciation for the improbability of our relationship grew. The differences never mattered. We found a spark in each other and it continued to glow for me for five decades.

The first day in Mrs. Blackstone's class set the tone for the rest of the semester and beyond. She assigned us to attend a meeting of the local city council and write a report on what we observed. I went to the council meeting the next night, wrote my report when I got home, and turned it in the following morning, though it wasn't due until the end of the week. I had five years of junior high and high school journalism behind me by then as well as three years "stringing" for five local newspapers. A report on a city council meeting was no challenge. Three years later, as a reporter at the local daily newspaper, I was being paid to report on meetings of that same city council.

The next few assignments didn't interest me, so I skipped them. About two weeks later, Mrs. Blackstone handed back the graded city council reports to everyone in the class but me. I raised my hand and asked for my report. She said she would give it back when I turned in my next assignment. She laughed; I laughed and everyone else in the class laughed. The games were on. This conservative woman and I were going to get along just fine.

The city council report became a joke that ran through the entire semester. One time I told her I didn't see any sense in doing another paper because she hadn't returned my council report and I needed to understand her standards and expectations before doing any additional assignments. Another time I told her I thought she wanted to keep the report because it would be worth a lot of money when I became a famous news reporter. I offered to autograph it for her.

Another study unit during that semester was called Family Life. Sex education was out of the question in the 1950s, so they called it "family life" and stayed far away from anything having to do with how to make a family. That was left for us to figure out in our cars at drive-in theaters.

I don't remember much of what we covered in that unit, but I do remember one day Mrs. Blackstone was delivering a lecture that included something about how to order a diaper service in those pre-Pampers days. I was looking out the window at the trees dancing in the autumn breeze, thinking about the football game coming up that Friday night, and paying not the slightest attention to what was going on in class. She stopped the lecture and said something like, "Larry, could you at least look like you're paying attention."

Without missing a beat, I answered, "I come from a long line of bachelors and I'm going to teach my kids the same thing. I won't need to know this stuff."

Any other teacher would have thrown me out of class. That conservative Christian missionary just shook her head and smiled. Usually, she could give as good as she took. This time she didn't respond. But she didn't blush either. She just resumed the lecture, only now everyone was awake.

One assignment that caught my interest called for us to write a paper on some aspect of family life. My paper was titled "Why the Institution of Marriage as Practiced Today Is Alien to the Human Spirit." It was a cynical, off-the-top-of-my-head discussion of the destructive nature of the sacrifice, accommodation, and compromise involved in marriage. I did no research for the paper; it was based on things I had been thinking for some time. I put the paper on Mrs. Blackstone's desk on my way out the door at the end of class the next day—a week ahead of the due date.

I showed up for class the following day expecting some reaction. I watched for some sign of recognition. I got back nothing. I thought, *Either she's taunting me by not taking the bait, or she hasn't looked at the paper yet.* This was only the second piece of work I turned in all semester other than tests and assignments we did in class. It was a title and subject that should have teased the curiosity of any teacher in the 1950s, let alone the advisor to the Campus Christian Club. She must have wondered enough to look at it. But she wasn't going to give me the satisfaction of a reaction.

When she handed the graded papers back some weeks later, mine included this time, my friend Bill looked at me with surprise and asked, "You did this one?"

I just smiled. "What [grade] did you get?" Bill asked. I showed him the front page of the paper. There was no grade, just a note in red pencil: "How do you know these things?" Bill read the title of the paper and the teacher's note. He started to laugh. Another friend, sitting at the desk in front of Bill, turned to see what was happening and Bill handed the paper to him.

As the paper circulated through the room, I raised my hand. Mrs. Blackstone smiled and asked what I wanted. "What kind of grade is this?" I asked.

"It's exactly what the paper deserves," she answered.

"What did you write in your grade book?" I asked.

"Nothing, yet," she answered. "I can't find your page. I don't use it often enough."

At the end of the hour, Mrs. Blackstone asked me to stay after class for a few minutes. She was concerned about some of the things she read in the paper. She asked if things were okay at home, if my parents were getting along. I told her everything was fine and by most measures they were getting along. She asked why I was so cynical about marriage and I said, "Look around. At least five kids in the class have parents who are divorced." Five out of 27 was pretty significant in the 1950s in working-class Burbank.

I turned in one more assignment that semester – the term paper. We were given one week to pick a topic and submit an outline. The only requirement was that it had to relate to something we studied during the semester. I submitted an outline for a paper titled "The Rise of Communism in China". I figured I had nothing to lose—I hadn't done enough work to establish a grade and I needed to pass the class to graduate. To challenge myself and my teacher I was going to research and write about something she had witnessed firsthand.

Mrs. Blackstone asked what the topic had to do with anything we studied. I reminded her we studied different forms of government and even though my paper had to do with national government in China instead of local government in the U.S., it was a form of government. Besides, I said, it was a subject in which I was interested and it was more interesting than most of the stuff we covered in Senior Problems. She approved the topic.

I worked hard on that paper, harder than anything else I had done in three years of high school. I skipped nights with my buddies at the local drive-in restaurant to devote time to the research. We had no Bing or Google back then, so when I told my parents I was going to the library, that's where I really went. The day I turned in the paper I knew I had done a good job. Mrs. Blackstone agreed and graded the paper an A. In some way, I guess, the selection of the topic was a way to tell her how much I respected her.

On the last day of school, Mrs. Blackstone took roll and then announced: "Now, a moment we've all been waiting for." She called me to the front of the classroom.

I walked hesitantly, sensing a prank. Mrs. Blackstone opened her desk drawer and took out some papers that were rolled up like a scroll and tied with a red ribbon. With great flare, she handed it to me. It was my city council report. The grade was an A. I did three assignments the entire semester and got an A on two of them and a curious handwritten note on the other. I also did well on all the in-class tests, passed the course and graduated.

I recalled some of these stories at that 50th anniversary lunch. She didn't remember them, of course. Nor did she remember any of us who were at the lunch. Why should she? Many hundreds of seventeen-year-old high school seniors had passed through her life after we did. But she appreciated that we cared enough to want to be with her again, and she told us so in a voice no different at 101 than I remembered it being in that classroom fifty years before.

Each of us said a few words about what it had meant to know her and how fondly we remembered her.

When it was my turn, I told the story of an incident that seemed to spark some recognition. It does as much as anything else to define the relationship we had. To get to Mrs. Blackstone's classroom I had to walk by the home economics room. One day the girls in the cooking class (yes, it was all girls) made trays of garlic bread, and the whole building smelled of garlic. I stuck my head into the room and one of the girls gave me a slice of bread. I asked for a tray and marched into Mrs. Blackstone's room with enough garlic bread for everyone in the class. What did Mrs. Blackstone do? She took the first slice. I don't know whether what I saw in her face when I recalled this incident over lunch was because she actually remembered, or whether she just knew that's what she would have done. I would have loved the opportunity for a more private talk with her, to hear how she felt about the Tiananmen Square protests and when she saw those photos of that Chinese boy standing defiantly in front of that line of tanks.

At the end of each school year, Mrs. Blackstone invited her graduating seniors to a Chinese dinner at her home. She taught us about some of the customs of China and how to use chopsticks. That made more sense than consigning her to teach us about diaper services in a Senior Problems class. She was a witness to history. That's what she should have been teaching.

Years later, when I taught my sons to use chopsticks, I told them about the remarkable woman who taught me. So her legacy is alive for at least one more generation. She smiled broadly when I told her that at the reunion lunch. Now, when I see my grandchildren learning to use chopsticks,

I tell them where I learned and of the special woman who taught me.

One of the women at the lunch at the Smoke House asked Mrs. Blackstone if she cooked those Chinese dinners herself. Sheepishly, she admitted, "Some years I did. Others I may have gone to Chinatown and brought food in." There were only about fifty-four of us in my senior class, and not all of us had Mrs. Blackstone as our teacher. Because we were a small group—only about twenty of us were at that dinner at her home—I would like to believe we were one of the classes for which she did the cooking herself.

I've loved Chinese food since I first tasted it as a young child in Brooklyn. When the dieticians told me after my coronary bypass surgery that I should stay out of Chinese restaurants because of the sodium content in the food, I was less than thrilled. So I developed my own recipes for dishes in which I can control the sodium. Here, in recognition of that wonderful teacher and the fun and respect we shared, are some of my recipes for Chinese dishes.

Chinese Style Roast Chicken

> 6 tablespoons low-sodium soy sauce
> 2 tablespoons sesame oil
> 1 tablespoon rice vinegar
> 2 tablespoons sweet sherry
> 1 teaspoon chili powder
> 1 tablespoon powdered ginger (or 1 teaspoon grated fresh ginger)
> 1 teaspoon turmeric
> 1/2 teaspoon Chinese five spice
> 1 teaspoon grated, dried orange peel (optional)
> 1 whole fryer chicken, about 3 1/2 to 4 pounds

Combine the first nine ingredients in a bowl and mix them together. Separate the skin from the chicken using your fingertips. With a teaspoon, spread the mixture under the skin and in the cavity of the chicken. Rub the chicken skin with some of the mixture. Let the chicken marinate several hours in the refrigerator.

Remove the chicken from the refrigerator a half hour before you are ready to begin roasting. Place the chicken, breast side down, on a rack in a roasting pan. Roast for 30 minutes in a preheated oven at 450 degrees. Reduce the heat to 400 degrees. Turn the chicken breast side up and continue roasting another 30 minutes. Remove the chicken from the oven, cover it loosely with tinfoil, and let it sit about 10 minutes so the juices can set. Cut the legs, thighs, and wings into separate pieces and slice the breast.

Serve with fried rice.

Serves four.

Chinese Roast Pork Two Ways

> Purchase either:
> 1 one-pound piece of pork tenderloin or
> 1 rib-end pork loin with the bone in (3-4 bones)

FOR THE PORK TENDERLOIN

Use the same marinade as for the roast chicken (previous page). Marinate the pork in the refrigerator 6–8 hours. Turn once at about 4 hours to assure both sides are immersed in the marinade. Preheat the oven to 325 degrees. Put the pork on a rack in a shallow roasting pan and roast for 35 minutes. Let the pork stand for 10 minutes before slicing. Slice about 1/4 inch thick on a diagonal across the grain of the meat.

Serves two.

FOR THE PORK LOIN

Increase the amount of marinade about 50 percent. Cut away most of the fat on the outside of the loin. With a sharp knife, cut a shallow cross pattern in the meat. Use the knife point to stab holes between the bones and in the ends of the roast. Place the loin in a pan and pour the marinade over it. Turn the loin so all sides are coated with the marinade, ending with the meat side down and the bones up. Spoon some marinade over the bones. Let the roast sit in the marinade in the refrigerator for several hours. Turn it occasionally to recoat the ends and spoon additional marinade over the bones.

Take the pork out of the refrigerator about 1/2 hour before you are ready to begin roasting. Preheat the oven to 325 degrees. Place the pork on a rack in a shallow roasting pan, and roast for 25 minutes per pound. (Unless you are going to wash it first, don't use the same roasting pan as you used to marinate the meat, or you will end up with a pan that is very difficult to clean.)

Remove the pork from the oven, cover it loosely with tinfoil, and let it stand for 10 minutes to seal in the juices. Using a sharp knife, cut the meat completely away from the bones and cut into 1/4 inch slices.

If I am serving just the family, I like to cut the bones apart and serve them with the meat on a platter. Chewing the meat from the bones is a real treat.

Note: This will give you pork that is still pink. I think it is more flavorful that way. If you want it beyond pink, increase the cooking time to 28 minutes per pound.

Serves four.

Both the pork tenderloin and the bone-in roast go well with baked sweet potatoes or yams, fried rice, or roasted russet potatoes.

Rumaki Spread

- 1/2 pound chicken livers
- 1/4 cup butter
- 2 tablespoons lemon juice
- 1 tablespoon low-sodium soy sauce
- 2 teaspoons brown sugar
- 4 scallions, chopped (divided)
- 1/2 teaspoon dry hot mustard
- ground ginger
- garlic salt
- 1 (5-ounce) can water chestnuts, drained and chopped
- 2 strips of bacon, fried to crisp and crumbled

Sauté the livers in butter until they are no longer pink in the middle. Cool the livers. Put the livers through a Foley grinder (food mill), or mash them well with a fork. Add the lemon juice, soy sauce, sugar, 1 teaspoon scallion, mustard, ginger and garlic salt to taste. Stir in the water chestnuts and bacon. Chill until ready to use. Allow the liver to return to room temperature. Garnish with additional scallions and serve with sesame crackers.

Fried Rice

> 2 tablespoons sesame oil
> 1/2 stalk celery, diced
> 1/4 cup chopped onion
> 1 teaspoon of water
> 1 tablespoon low-sodium soy sauce
> 1 egg
> 3/4 cup long-grain cooked white rice
> 1/4 cup frozen peas, cooked to package directions
> 1/4 cup chopped scallions

Heat the oil in a 2-quart saucepan. Add the celery and onions and sauté until softened. Remove the celery and onions from the pan. Beat the water and soy sauce into the egg. Add the egg to the pan and scramble it with a spatula. When the egg is scrambled, add the celery, onions, and cooked rice to the pan. Add the cooked peas and sauté over medium-low heat, stirring frequently to prevent sticking, until the rice is heated through. Stir in the scallions.

Serves two as a side dish with main course.

To turn this into Shrimp Fried Rice, buy 1/4 pound of cooked bay shrimp and add them at room temperature to the rice for the last 5 minutes of cooking.

Sui Mai

> 1/2 pound raw shrimp, peeled, cleaned, and chopped very fine
> 1/2 pound ground pork
> 1/2 cup finely diced bok choy (white part only)
> 4 dried black mushrooms, soaked to soften and diced
> 1 1/2 tablespoons fresh ginger, minced
> 1 clove garlic, minced
> 1 egg white
> 2 tablespoons low-sodium soy sauce
> 1 tablespoon cornstarch
> 1 teaspoon sesame oil
> wonton skins
> dipping sauce (see following page)

Combine the first ten ingredients in a bowl. Mix gently but thoroughly. Place the mixture in the refrigerator for about 1 hour.

Place one rounded teaspoon of the mixture in the middle of each wonton skin. Gather the sides of the skin around the filling, leaving the top open. Place the folded skins in a single layer on a steamer rack. Cover and steam over rapidly boiling water about 5–6 minutes. Serve hot with dipping sauce.

Makes about three dozen dumplings.

Dipping Sauce

> 1/4 cup low-sodium soy sauce
> 2 tablespoons rice vinegar
> 1/2 teaspoon sesame oil
> 1 1/2 teaspoons fresh ginger, minced
> 1/2 teaspoon finely sliced chives

Combine all the ingredients in a glass bowl. Let stand at room temperature several hours to give the flavors a chance to blend.

Chicken or Shrimp Chop Suey

1 1/2 tablespoons sesame oil
1 cup boneless, skinless chicken thigh, sliced thin
or 1 cup raw shrimp cut in small pieces but not chopped*
1 cup sliced white mushrooms
1 teaspoon salt
4 teaspoons low-sodium soy sauce, divided
1 cup celery slices, cut into 1/2 inch pieces
1/4 pound bean sprouts
1/2 pound Chinese greens (bok choy, cabbage, etc.), coarsely chopped
2/3 cup water, divided
2 teaspoons cornstarch

Heat the oil in a wok or a wide frying pan until very hot. Add the chicken or shrimp, mushrooms and salt. Sauté, stirring constantly, for 2 minutes. Add 1 teaspoon of soy sauce and the celery, sprouts and greens. Stir and cook for 3 minutes. Add 1/3 cup of water, cover and cook for 3 minutes. Mix the cornstarch into the remaining 1/3 cup of water until dissolved. Stir the remaining 3 teaspoons of soy sauce into the cornstarch. Add the cornstarch to the chop suey and stir until the gravy reaches the desired consistency.

Serve with steamed white rice.

A variation can use thinly sliced beef or pork in place of the chicken or shrimp.

Serves two.

Chicken Chow Mein

> 4 tablespoons vegetable oil
> 1 cup shredded Chinese cabbage (or combination of cabbage and bok choy)
> 3 cups thinly sliced celery
> 1 pound bean sprouts
> 1 (4-ounce) can water chestnuts
> 1 (4-ounce) can bamboo shoots
> 1 teaspoon salt
> 1/4 teaspoon black pepper
> 2 cups chicken broth
> 2 1/2 teaspoons cornstarch
> 1/4 cup water
> 1/4 cup low-sodium soy sauce
> 2 cups cooked chicken thighs, cut into bite-size pieces*
> Chinese fried noodles

Heat the oil in a wok or wide frying pan until very hot. Add the cabbage, celery, bean sprouts, water chestnuts and bamboo shoots. Stir quickly to coat with the oil. Add the salt and pepper. Stir in the chicken broth and cook, uncovered, about 10 minutes. Mix together the cornstarch, water and soy sauce. Add the cornstarch mixture to the pan and stir until the sauce thickens. Add the chicken and heat thoroughly. Serve with Chinese fried noodles.

You can substitute shrimp or pork for the chicken.

Serve with steamed or fried rice.

Serves four.

Inspiration Shrimp

I entered the market on the way home from work one day with no idea what I would make for dinner. As I strolled by the fish counter, I spotted some beautiful shrimp. I was in the mood for something Chinese, so I grabbed some scallions. At home, I pulled all the other ingredients from the pantry and produced this dish. Jennifer called it "inspired." Thus the name—Inspiration Shrimp.

> 3/4 pound medium shell-on shrimp
> 2 cups plus 3 tablespoons water, divided
> 2 tablespoons butter
> 3 tablespoons cornstarch
> 1 large garlic clove, minced
> 1/4 teaspoon red pepper flakes
> 1 teaspoon ground ginger
> 2 large scallions

Peel and clean the shrimp. Put the shrimp shells in a saucepan with 2 cups of the water. Boil slowly for about 20 minutes. Using a fine strainer, pour the broth into a measuring cup and discard the shells.

Melt the butter in a 10-inch frying pan. Mix together the cornstarch, 3 tablespoons of water and 1 tablespoon of the hot shrimp broth.

Add the garlic, 1 cup of shrimp broth, the red pepper flakes, and ginger to the frying pan. Stir in enough cornstarch mixture to thicken the broth. Alternately, add more broth and more cornstarch until it's all in the pan. Add the shrimp and scallions. Mix well into the sauce. Cover and cook over medium-low heat for about 3 minutes. Remove the cover, stir, and let cook uncovered until the shrimp are cooked through, about 2 more minutes.

Serve over steamed rice or with fried rice.

Serves two.

CHAPTER SEVEN
Forever Seventeen

A TEENAGE ADVENTURE
It happened long ago beside a river—a stolen day away from school became a teenage infatuation that has never been forgotten.

On the road from pubescent titillation to full-fledged romantic love, there's a wonderful, sometimes bumpy side trip through teenage infatuation. My journey along that detour started on a day when the Southern California air was so clear, the sky so blue, the sun so bright, the temperature so warm and the view so spectacular that we might have been living in a Technicolor movie filmed with sound-stage perfection.

It was one of those days when you can look across the Los Angeles basin from the Hollywood Freeway near the landmark Capitol Records Building in Hollywood and see the Pacific Ocean more than twenty miles away. If you look the other way, you can see every window glistening at far-off City Hall. That kind of day came infrequently in 1955. We get more of them now, as we are winning the battle against the layers of brown smog that once choked us and forced children to stay indoors during recess at school.

The adventure started with four of us sitting in my friend Phil's car in front of the high school, waiting for the bell to call us to class. Four teenage guys in a 1947 Chevy convertible on a glorious spring morning with the school year winding down—a prescription for almost anything but going to class.

Phil put the feeling into words when he suggested cutting school. But his intended destination was not the beach, as would have been expected on a beautiful Southern California day. Instead, Phil wanted to go a hundred miles north to Bakersfield, to see a girlfriend named Barbara.

In a heartbeat I said I would go with him. (Actually, we didn't say "in a heartbeat" back then, but that's how long it took me to agree.) Dave and Rich chose to stay behind.

With the convertible top down and the radio on, Phil aimed the car toward Highway 99—the old road north through the Tehachapi Mountains. Most of the route was a four-lane road back then, two in each direction. For some stretches it was one lane each way with a passing lane in the middle. The notoriously dangerous, curvy road rose and dropped along the contours of the mountains, winding through majestic geologic formations and fragrant wooded areas. Fields of wildflowers—purple, yellow, and orange, and brush strokes of lavender—painted the hillsides and danced in the breeze.

A mega highway and a large dam wiped out the old road in the early 1970s. The new road—Interstate 5—skims along the tops of the mountains, and most of the best views have been lost. Today, drivers barrel along at 80 miles an hour and still risk having an 18-wheeler run up their rear end.

It was midmorning when we pulled into a curbside parking spot on the Bakersfield High School campus. As Phil turned off the engine, he spotted Barbara, not fifteen feet in front of us.

"There she is," he said as he jumped out of the car and called to her. I watched as they talked for just a few seconds. Then Barbara walked away, and Phil returned to the car.

"She's going to get a friend for you," he told me.

Soon two lovely girls were walking toward us—Barbara and her friend Lynne—their dusty-blonde ponytails bobbing behind them. I got out of the car so Barbara could sit up front with Phil. Lynne and I sat in the back.

I couldn't take my eyes off her. I had been with girls before: at the beach, in the park, at a movie theater. But never like this—never on a stolen adventure far from home with a girl a year older than I was, never with one so lovely and mature. We had to lean in close to be heard as we talked in the wind-whipped rear seat of the car. Lynne looked into my eyes as she spoke. She chatted and laughed as if we were old friends. She asked about our day and whether I had my driver's license yet. She touched my arm with an air of familiarity when I said something funny.

At Barbara's house, Lynne changed into a borrowed pink-and-white checked boat-neck blouse and white shorts. If I noticed what Barbara was wearing, I certainly can't recall it now.

We drove to a remote spot along the Kern River. Phil and Barbara walked off along the banks and left us alone. Lynne spread a blanket on the sand and sat down. I sat on a boulder close by. We talked for a while, small talk about how we knew Phil and Barbara. Then she lay back on the blanket and closed her eyes.

Flecks of sunlight dropped through the filter of the trees and danced between the shadows that covered her. I wasn't sure what to do. After a few minutes, she seemed to sense me looking at her. She opened her eyes, smiled, and patted the blanket in a signal for me to join her. We listened to the sounds of leaves rustling in the breeze and the river rushing by, swelled by the springtime thaw in the nearby Sierra Nevada Mountains.

I've taken that ride over the Tehachapi Mountains scores of times since that day, on the old road and the new one. The feeling of youth and adventure echoes to me from the mountains and fields every time.

It all happened so long ago, more than sixty years ago. Yet I remember so clearly the enthusiasm with which she greeted me when we were introduced, the fullness of her mouth and softness of her eyes, and a song we heard on the radio: "Every day, I fall in love all over again with you."

I was completely taken by her—a teenage boy with a

girl different from any he had known before, a girl with the confidence of a budding woman, the soon-to-be college student who was displacing the high school girl she had been. No endless chatter to fill every second, just peace and contentment as we lay quietly by the river in the springtime sun.

Life has taken me many miles since that day by the river. Years later, on the anniversary of the day I met Lynne, I took a drive over the mountain to the place by the river where we had been. I sat on the sand alone and watched the water in its never-ending rush out of the Sierras. I smelled the trees and let the silence embrace me in that place where we will be forever seventeen.

I was browsing Classmates.com a few years ago, entering names of people from bygone times. I found Lynne's name there along with a photo from her high school yearbook. She lives no more than forty-five minutes from me in L.A. I stared at the computer screen, tempted to send her a message—to see if she remembers, to see whether she would like to have a cup of coffee.

I didn't do it. The memory is enough. What if she didn't remember me, or that special day?

I've been in Bakersfield many times through the years. When our sons were in elementary school, we took them to Inter-Tribal Indian Festivals at the Fair Grounds. I ran election campaigns for local candidates and ballot measures; I attended football games and track meets at the Bakersfield College stadium and basketball games in the gym.

I have a warm spot in my heart for that city because of a girl named Lynne. She represented my coming of age, the bridge between teenage infatuation and the doorstep of bachelorhood.

Many times, when I visited Bakersfield, I would have dinner at one of the city's wonderful Basque restaurants. To recall that day by the river and the girl who made it so memorable, here is a recipe for a dish you are likely to find at one of Bakersfield's fine Basque restaurants.

Basque Chicken

1/4 cup olive oil
1 cup all-purpose flour
1/2 teaspoon salt
1/4 teaspoon freshly ground black pepper
8 chicken parts, legs or thighs
4 large tomatoes, peeled, seeded, and chopped
4 ounces of lean ham, diced
1 (4-ounce) jar pimientos, drained and sliced
1/2 cup dry white wine
chopped fresh parsley for garnish

Preheat the oven to 350 degrees. Heat the oil in a large frying pan. Combine the flour, salt and pepper in a medium bowl. Dredge the chicken pieces in the flour mixture. Shake off any excess flour. Brown the chicken on all sides in the oil. Transfer the chicken to a 3- or 4-quart casserole with a tight-fitting lid.

Drain the oil from the frying pan. Add the tomatoes and ham and cook over medium heat about 5 minutes, stirring frequently. Stir in the pimientos. Add the wine and simmer 3 to 4 minutes. Pour the mixture over the chicken in the casserole. Cover and bake until the chicken is cooked through, about 45 minutes. Garnish with chopped parsley and serve over rice.

Serves four.

CHAPTER EIGHT

Convertible Cars and Celebrity Bars

THE "GEE WHIZ" YEARS
Here I am with singer, songwriter and actress Marti Barris in 1960, at a Louie Prima and Keely Smith concert at the Moulin Rouge nightclub in Hollywood. Our fathers knew each other in New York. Marti and I attended high school together in Los Angeles.

When we're young, we can believe that whatever happens never happened before—to anyone. With little experience to lend perspective, everything is larger than large and more dramatic. Love is more "real" and more "forever". Until it ends. Then no one ever hurt so much.

The first time you want to break up with someone, you go through hell, delaying, trying to figure out how to do it, what to say. It doesn't get easier the next time, not if you have a heart and ever really cared about the person. Then, when someone breaks up with you, you know you'll never love again. Later, you learn life actually does go on.

After those days of youthful drama, the time comes to hone the lessons learned and ride them into maturity. For me, those were my bachelor years of the late 1950s and the 1960s in an enchanted place called Los Angeles, a paradise for young single people. It was a time before rampant drug use and conspicuous self-absorption, before bodyguards and rude public behavior and street gangs and guns and HIV, when restaurants were quiet and elegant and people dressed for an evening out. It was a time to drive convertible cars and hang out in celebrity bars, a time of freedom to taste the pleasures of life without greed or complication.

They were my "gee-whiz" years.

Gee whiz! I met Natalie Wood, the stunning actress, waiting for an elevator in a building in Beverly Hills. We chatted briefly in the elevator and got out on the same floor to go to the same suite of offices. I teased her and asked if she was following me. She laughed. No security guards around her. Just two young, single people in an elevator headed for the same *Life* magazine office, sharing friendly banter. I will never understand why I didn't ask her to dinner.

Gee whiz! I met Tuesday Weld, the brash and extremely sexy young actress, at a crap table in Las Vegas one night in the early 1960s. We watched a lounge show together, then went our separate ways.

Gee whiz! I knew Bobby Troup and Julie London, and they knew me, because I hung out at the China Trader restaurant and bar in Toluca Lake along with so many celebrities of the music industry.

Gee whiz! I got my first experience in the lures of infidelity with the wife of an acquaintance. She married young, resented her role as housebound wife and mother, and turned to me for an adventure.

There were endless gee whizzes in those years, when my job as a news reporter and columnist gave me access to the places, people and events that defined an exciting time.

For several years I was the volunteer executive director of a local preliminary to the Miss America Pageant. Among other duties, I had to counsel contestants whose talent was not always up to the songs they were planning to sing, whose boyfriends resented their participation, whose parents were pushing too hard, or whose evening gowns were not flattering.

I saw beautiful and talented young women up close at their best and worst. In the long hours of rehearsals, in the various public and private settings and in the wash of emotional highs and lows, I discovered many of the divine complexities that make up a woman. I was there to participate, but I also observed. I never dated a contestant during the competition. After it was over, however, I was free to ask and they were free to accept or decline. I asked just twice; they accepted both times.

Along the way, I discovered the world of thrills that can live in the eyes of a woman, and oh, what magic there is if you are the man at whom she is looking. We've all known it—all of us guys. We've all felt it—that look that says, "I want to be held, now; I want to be kissed, now; I want to touch you, now."

Most of my best friends throughout my life have been girls or women. I like women better, trust them more, and find them more open, accepting, and honest than men. Women smile more easily, more often, and more genuinely. They are easier to talk to and confide in; they listen better and compete less. There are exceptions, of course, and I have known a few of them, too.

As for men, I tend to not like them in groups of more than one. As soon as there are two or more, the competition begins and crudeness can creep in.

Watch two women in a restaurant, their cell phones tucked away in their purses. Notice how involved they can be with each other, how focused they are on the conversation. Watch how easily they gesture with a hand or a tilt of the head. Watch the many kinds of smiles they exchange and the expressiveness of their eyes. See the intimacy.

Put two men in that same restaurant and they just might spend the entire meal without either of them smiling. They will talk without looking at each other. Their eyes will be scanning the room, probably sneaking looks at the two women in the previous paragraph. Often it goes beyond sneaking looks to outright ogling.

After the early years of youth and before the tender times of more complete love, there was a time to touch life and run among its fields with no expectations—the Vegas nights, the Palm Springs days, the trips to Mexico City and Acapulco and New York and San Francisco. Those were the times to date without needing to love, to love without needing to commit, and to enjoy the company of a woman for her own wonderful sake.

I remember dinners at La Mer on the beach near Malibu, operas at the Dorothy Chandler Pavilion, afternoons at Santa Anita racetrack, evening jaunts to Las Vegas after work for dinner and to see Louie Prima and Keely Smith, and a quick trip to New York for a performance of *Camelot*. I remember late-night strolls around Echo Park Lake, frozen mornings in a cabin at Big Bear Lake, motor boats on Lake Arrowhead, dinners at L.A.'s finest restaurants and nights at the Academy Awards.

Those were golden years and carefree days, when memories were made to be recalled and retold. I remember the names and faces of so many of the women who accompanied me through those "gee-whiz" years. I remember the circumstances that brought many of us together for the sometimes glamorous, sometimes frivolous, sometimes tender moments we shared. To all of you who allowed me into your lives and who passed through my life, I salute you and thank you, wherever life has taken you. You remain very much a part of me. You set the table for everything that came after.

At the height of my "gee-whiz" years, two friends and I rented a house. We divided the domestic chores among us. Jim was responsible for the inside of the house: dusting, vacuuming, washing and drying the dishes, etc. Brian was responsible for the outside: mowing the lawns, cleaning the droppings from the olive trees, and all other exterior maintenance. The kitchen was my domain. I was responsible for making sure the house was stocked with what was needed for breakfasts and lunches and for preparing dinners for the three of us and any dates who might be invited to join us.

Sunday morning breakfasts were legendary at our bachelor house. If there was a party in the house Saturday night, Sunday breakfast would include whoever stayed over and crashed on the floor or couches. And there were the friends who knew if they stopped by, they would be fed.

It was wild in my kitchen on those Sunday mornings. The novelty of a man cooking drew many of the wives and dates of our friends to the kitchen as spectators or as volunteers who wanted to help. Untold dozens of eggs were sacrificed with unbridled enthusiasm as I tried to prove there really is no limit to the variety of fillings and toppings that can go into an omelet.

Here are a few of the breakfast recipes rooted in those bachelor days.

About Omelets

There should be no such thing as a recipe for an omelet. Maybe directions on how to assemble one, but an omelet should be as good as the cook who creates it. If that sounds intimidating, don't let it be. You know what you like, the tastes and flavors you prefer, what meats, cheeses and vegetables you favor. That's all you need to become a good omelet cook.

Instead of a detailed, step-by-step recipe for omelets, I'm going to give you some guidelines and hints. If you have any creative instincts at all and any appreciation for the tastes of different combinations of foods and herbs and spices, you will get more satisfaction from concocting your own signature omelets than you ever could from following someone else's recipe. And the more omelets you concoct, the more you will learn for the next time.

THE EGG PART

> 3 eggs
> 1 teaspoon orange juice*
> 1 tablespoon carbonated water (cold tap water will do if you have no carbonated water)
> 1 teaspoon milk
> 1/4 teaspoon salt
> 1/4 teaspoon ground black pepper (optional)
> herbs (according to style of omelet and your taste)
> 2 tablespoons butter

Put the eggs, orange juice, water, milk, salt and pepper into a bowl. Using a whisk or fork, beat the eggs until they are light and frothy. Add the herbs to the egg mixture and stir in well.

Melt the butter in an omelet pan. Set the heat at medium-low, and pour the eggs into the pan.

When the eggs have set slightly, put the fillings over one half of the eggs. (See suggested fillings below.) From time to time, lift an edge of the egg and tilt the pan so the runny part of the egg can spill over the edge. When the eggs are almost totally set around the edges but still moist in the center, use a spatula to fold the eggs in half. Serve as is or with toppings. (See other list below.)

I have no idea what the orange juice accomplishes or where I got the idea to add it. It's probably something I read a long time ago. If I don't have any fresh orange juice handy, I skip this ingredient. I know the juice deepens the color of the omelet, but I can't say with certainty that it alters the taste.

FILLINGS AND TOPPINGS

Most of my omelets are created on the spot based on my mood and the ingredients at hand. I don't think I've ever made the same filling the same way twice, even on those mornings when I was turning out omelets for a crowd. This is your chance to show off. Take a chance. Use combinations of these ingredients as fillings, toppings, or stirred into the egg mixture. As your omelet skills grow, add your own ideas for fillings and toppings.

Among the ingredients you may want to consider in any combination that sounds good to you are the following:

- cheddar cheese
- Jack cheese
- Swiss cheese
- chopped ham

- cooked sausage (cut-up links or crumbled)
- cooked turkey
- cooked shrimp
- cooked ground beef
- onion: raw, sautéed, or stewed
- sun-dried tomatoes, folded into the egg mixture
- herbs for an ethnic bent (oregano or basil for Italian, cumin for something Mexican, herbs de Provence for a French style, etc.) stirred into the egg mixture before cooking
- scallions, chopped and either mixed into the eggs, folded into the omelet, or used as a topping
- tomatoes, diced or sliced, raw or sautéed, either folded into the omelet or used as a topping
- sliced mushrooms, sautéed, either folded into the omelet or used as a topping
- avocado, best sliced as a topping
- salsa, as a topping

LEO (Lox, Eggs, and Onions)

> 1 tablespoon butter
> 1/2 cup onions cut in half rings
> 1/2 cup small pieces of a good quality lox
> 3 eggs, beaten
> 1 tablespoon carbonated water (cold tap water if you have no carbonated water)
> black pepper to taste

Heat the butter in a frying pan until very hot. Reduce the heat to medium. Add the onions and stir until well browned. If you have enough time—maybe even the day before—stew the onions so they are well browned and sweet. Reduce the heat to medium-low. Add the lox pieces and stir with the onions about 1 minute. With a whisk, beat the carbonated water and pepper into the eggs. Pour the eggs into the pan with the onions and lox. Scramble the eggs until done to taste.

Serve with fried potatoes, hash browns, or roasted potatoes and a bagel with cream cheese.

Serves one.

Eggs Creole

> 1/4 pound pork sausage links, cut in bite-size pieces
> 1 (3-ounce) can tomato paste
> 2/3 cup water
> 1/4 cup minced bell pepper (any color you prefer)
> 1/4 cup diced onion
> 5 eggs
> 5 tablespoons milk
> salt and pepper to taste
> 4 slices toasted bread

Brown the sausage pieces in a saucepan. Pour off the excess fat. Add the tomato paste, water, bell pepper, and onions. Simmer 5 minutes to make a sauce.

In a bowl, beat together the eggs, milk, salt and pepper. Scramble the eggs in a greased or buttered frying pan over medium heat. Place a portion of eggs on each slice of toast. Spoon the sauce over the eggs.

Serves four.

Breakfast Potatoes

> 1 medium russet potato
> 1/4 cup butter (or more if needed)
> 1/2 cup diced onion
> 1/2 cup chopped red bell pepper (optional)
> salt and pepper to taste

Scrub the potato but do not peel. Cut the potato into cubes of about one inch. Put the cubed potato in a saucepan with enough water to cover. Bring to a boil and cook at a moderate boil about 8 minutes, until the potatoes are soft but not mushy. Check the potatoes with the point of a knife for doneness. Remove the potatoes from the water and rinse under cold water. Drain the potatoes thoroughly and pat them dry with a paper towel.

Heat the butter in a frying pan until very hot. Add the potatoes, onions and peppers. Reduce the heat to medium. Stir the potatoes to coat with butter. Sprinkle with salt and pepper. Sauté until browned to taste. Stir frequently to prevent burning.

As a variation, you might want to mix about 1/4 teaspoon of chili powder into the butter before adding the potatoes.

Serves two.

Leftover Pork Roast Hash

> 1/2 brown onion, diced very small
> olive oil (not extra virgin)
> 1/2 russet potato, peeled and diced into 1/4 inch cubes
> 2 tablespoons butter
> salt and pepper to taste
> 1/2 pound leftover pork loin, cut into 1/4 inch cubes
> 2 large eggs

Brown the onions in olive oil; then set them aside.

Boil the potatoes 4 minutes, until the raw taste is gone, then drain thoroughly to dry. In the same pan in which you browned the onions, sauté the potatoes in butter, adding salt and black pepper, until the potatoes are lightly browned.

Add the pork and onions to the pan to heat.

Fry the eggs. Spoon the hash onto two plates and top each with a fried egg.

Serves two.

CHAPTER NINE
Marna's Time

WITH MARNA
It was the love that was going to last forever. Then it ended. Here we are, Marna and me, at the Cocoanut Grove nightclub in Los Angeles for opening night of an Eddie Fisher show in July, 1965.

A light rain was falling the night Marna came into my life. For the next eight months she made the sun shine. Then she left and I was changed in ways I never could have imagined.

Marna was the first woman I ever thought of as a permanent part of my life, and even though I never spoke with her after she ended our romance, she remains now, and always will be an indelible presence.

We met because of the persistence of my late sister, Myrna, who kept telling me about "someone I work with, who you should meet," until I finally gave in.

Marna certainly didn't need to be fixed up with me or anyone else. Her unforgettable smile was like a million sparkling diamonds in the twilight of a Los Angeles day. Her eyes were alive and alert. She laughed easily, spoke confidently and carried herself with assurance. She was intelligent and quick and absolutely beautiful. At least, that's the way I remember her and in my mind I have the freedom to keep her that way. She told me after we were together a few months, that she, too, had resisted our meeting until Myrna wore her down.

I stopped dating others as soon as we met. I wanted to spend every possible moment with her, and I showed her that in a hundred different ways. She knew how much I looked forward to seeing her each evening after work. She knew how I enjoyed doing special things for her and with her.

Soon, we were very much in love. We laughed and smiled and skipped across the landscape of Los Angeles for eight glorious months. Opening nights at the Cocoanut Grove nightclub in the glamorous Ambassador Hotel. Dinners at Scandia and other jewels of the L.A. restaurant world. Weekends in Palm Springs. Holidays in Mexico. Shows at The Crescendo and The Interlude. The crossword puzzles we did together over Sunday breakfast at her place or mine. For a time, it was enough.

It was a love affair I believed would last forever. Then it ended. After eight months, she sent me out of her life. She told me she knew someday I would want to have children and she was never going to have children. I never stopped wondering how she could have known that about me at a time when I hadn't even considered it. But she was right; she knew me better than I knew myself. I've wondered, also, how she could have been so sure about herself. But the proof is in the fact that she never did have children or marry.

Through the years I've thought a million times of the interlude of Marna in my life and the way it ended. I've thought how strange it seems that through our eight months together—with all the glory and the wonder and the magic of our time—the thought that we might marry never crossed my mind. Neither did the idea that there ever would be a time when we would no longer be together. I loved her. But I was too young and too wrapped up in being a bachelor to discover all the ways in which I loved her, or to show them to her. That kind of love comes later, with a maturity I had not yet achieved. I just knew with every fiber of my being that I adored her and wanted to be with her. And she knew it. We were spending every evening and weekend together and I was at the point of suggesting that we find an apartment to share. She ended our romance before I could do that.

Two people can ride the magic carpet of infatuation for a time. But eventually the carpet must land somewhere. Ours didn't land—it crashed before our relationship ever touched the depths of who we were or the heights of what it might have become.

What's strange is that, while I recall so many of the things we did and places we went, I can't remember much of what we talked about during our many hours together. But I do remember some of the things about which we *didn't* talk, and they seem equally strange.

We met one year after President John F. Kennedy was assassinated, but I don't recall ever speaking of how we felt about that. The United States' involvement in Vietnam was escalating and antiwar demonstrations and teach-ins were growing on college campuses. The free-speech movement and anti-draft actions in Berkeley, and the civil rights movement in the south were filling the news, but we never talked about any of those. I was a political reporter for a news-wire service and she was a casting agent in the movie and TV industry. But we never talked about our jobs. How can two people spend so much time together and never really get to know all the parts of each other?

On the other hand, there were all the good things that defined us as a couple. One day, we were driving to Baja California (Mexico) for the Memorial Day holiday weekend. Near San Diego, traffic came to a stop. We took a deck of cards from the glove compartment and sat calmly in the middle of the highway, with the top down on my Pontiac LeMans, and we played gin rummy until traffic started to flow again. Then there was the night at the Greek Theater, when we laughed so hard at a performance of *How to Succeed in Business Without Really Trying* that by intermission our cheeks hurt and we stood by our seats, massaging each other's face and laughing even more. There were all those nights we sat together and watched *The Tonight Show Starring Johnny Carson* and his guests. We laughed at the same jokes and liked the same entertainers. I look at some of the old photos of us at nightclubs and I see two people who were in love, who enjoyed being together, were completely at ease with each other and shared an appreciation for where they were and what they were doing. That must count for something.

When Marna told me she was ending our relationship, I was stunned. How could that happen? How could two people drift apart to the point where one wants to break up, yet the other isn't even aware of the drift? There had to be signs. There must have been signs. But I didn't see them then and, no matter how hard or how long I looked for them later, I never did find them, until ultimately I accepted that the reason she gave me was the real reason.

All that doesn't matter now. All that matters is that I loved Marna the only way and as much as I could at the time. But it wasn't the way she wanted to be loved or needed to be loved, and so she ended it.

I suppose every man has a Marna somewhere in his life, and every woman has a Jim, or Joe, or Larry. They stand unchanged through the years, neither tainted by the trials of time nor textured by a life of shared events. They are the embodiment of our youth and the fiction of our immortality.

Would I want to see Marna again if I could? Would I want to have dinner with her and see her smile again? Of course I would. I would like to thank her for being smart enough for both of us all those years ago and ask her how she knew before I did that having children would be important to me. I would love to ask how her life has gone. I hope the answer would be that she, too, has known fulfillment and that she remembers our time together with fondness. Of course, I can't be in love with her anymore. But I always will be in love with the time we had together.

POST SCRIPT

On May 27, 2011, I received an email from Marna's brother. He told me she had died one week earlier. In time I came to realize that the satisfaction I feel knowing that I loved her and she loved me is far greater than the sadness I felt when we broke up. When I look at photos of us together, I can smile at what was, with no regrets. This chapter was written and rewritten many times over the years as I thought about my time with Marna. It has been virtually unchanged since I learned of her death, other than to acknowledge the fact of that sad occurrence.

Scandia was one of my favorite restaurants even before I met Marna. To drive along Sunset Boulevard toward Scandia on a warm summer evening with the top down on the car ... To look across the Los Angeles basin on a clear evening and see the place where the sun was about to dip into the sea ... To watch the neon lights come on over the night clubs, bars and restaurants—Dino's, the Crescendo, the Interlude ... To be young in this place, on this boulevard, in the company of a wonderful woman ... To pull into the driveway and be greeted by parking attendants as a friend and served by a waiter who considered me one of his regulars ... What an eloquent statement about the time and the place.

Of all the memories I hold dear of my time with Marna, some of the most cherished are the times we were at Scandia. Those were the times that celebrated who we were as a couple—dressed well, dining well, smiling, laughing, enjoying the finest life had to offer in our magic city.

Scandia remained a favorite of mine after Marna and I parted. Jennifer and I dined there frequently; we took our two sons to Scandia while they were still very young. We also went there with Jennifer's sister and brother-in-law. We made our own memories, and we speak of them often. Though Scandia has been gone for many years, those memories live on.

The signature dish on the Scandia menu was the Viking Sword. What a showy and romantic presentation – served for two, carried across the room *en flambé* by the waiter. I would love to be able to provide the recipe for that meal, or some derivation of it. But I would have no idea where to turn for it. Besides, it wouldn't be a practical thing to try at home—pieces of beef, pork, and chicken *en brochette*, flaming away while held aloft on a giant sword. It would set off every smoke detector in the house. Instead, here are some recipes for other favorite dishes we enjoyed at Scandia.

Scandia Style Appetizer Meatballs

> 1/2 cup fresh bread crumbs
> 2 cups milk, divided
> 1/2 pound twice-ground beef or veal
> 1/2 pound twice-ground pork
> 1 egg
> 1 teaspoon salt
> 1/4 teaspoon pepper
> pinch of allspice
> 1/2 cup diced onion
> 2 tablespoons butter
> 1/4 cup clarified butter
> flour

Soak the bread crumbs in 1/2 cup milk until softened. Drain the milk from the bread crumbs. Combine the moistened crumbs with the beef, pork, egg, salt, pepper and allspice. Sauté the onions in the butter until they are tender and add them to the meat. Heat 1/2 cup of milk to lukewarm. Knead the meat mixture with your fingers while slowly adding the 1/2 cup of lukewarm milk. Chill until the mixture is firm enough to roll into meatballs.

Heat the clarified butter in a frying pan. Add the meatballs and fry until cooked through. Remove the meatballs from the pan. Drain off the fat. Dust the meatballs lightly with flour and return them to the pan. Add the remaining cup of milk* for a gravy and simmer a few minutes. Taste the gravy and adjust seasoning.

You may substitute broth or consommé for the milk in making the gravy with good results.

Makes fifty to sixty appetizer-size meatballs

Gazpacho Like Scandia Used to Make

Soup
4 large tomatoes, chunked
1 large onion, chunked
1 garlic clove, minced
1 large cucumber, peeled, seeded, and sliced
1 green bell pepper, seeded and diced
1 red bell pepper, seeded and diced
2 cups tomato juice
1/2 cup each red wine vinegar and white wine
1 1/2 tablespoons olive oil
2 tablespoons paprika
1 teaspoon salt
1 teaspoon freshly ground black pepper
1/2 teaspoon ground cumin
1/2 teaspoon chili powder
1 eggplant, baked (see below) and divided
Salt and ground black pepper to taste
4 tablespoons olive oil

Place all the soup ingredients except the eggplant, salt, and pepper in a large bowl and let stand at room temperature at least 2 hours so flavors can blend.

Wash the eggplant, slice it into 1/2 inch circles, leaving the skin on. Sprinkle both sides with salt, pepper and garlic powder. Pour the olive oil into a large, shallow roasting pan. Heat the oil in the oven at 450 degrees. When the oil is very hot, reduce the heat to 325 degrees. Put the eggplant slices in the hot oil and return the pan to the oven. Roast the eggplant for about 15 minutes. Turn the slices and roast another 15 minutes. Remove from the oven and let stand to cool. Remove the skin from the eggplant. Chop half the eggplant for the soup and cut the other half into cubes for the garnish.

Place all the soup ingredients, including one half of the eggplant, in a blender and liquefy. Cover and chill in the refrigerator at least one hour. Serve in soup bowls. Top with a dollop of sour cream, if desired.

> **Garnish**
> 1 medium cucumber, peeled, seeded and diced
> 1 avocado, peeled and diced
> 1/2 of the baked eggplant
> 4 slices French bread, toasted and diced
> sour cream (optional)

Serve cucumber, avocado, remaining eggplant, and bread in separate bowls as garnish.

Serves four.

Gravlaks a la Scandia

> 1 (2-pound) piece of salmon, skin left on
> 3 tablespoons salt
> 3 tablespoons sugar
> 1 tablespoon crushed black peppercorns
> 1/2 bunch dill

Cut the salmon in half lengthwise. Place one half, skin side down, in a baking dish. Rub with half the salt, sugar and peppercorns. Cover with dill sprigs. Rub the other half of the salmon with the remaining salt, sugar, and peppercorns, and lay this piece skin side up over the other piece of salmon. Wrap well in tinfoil or plastic wrap. Place a weighted plate on top of the fish.

Refrigerate for 48 hours, turning the fish every 12 hours. Each time you turn the fish, separate the two pieces and baste them with the pan liquids. Then rewrap tightly. When ready to serve, scrape off all the dill and seasonings. Place the fish skin side down on a cutting board and slice it very thinly on the diagonal, cutting away from the skin.

Scandia would cut the skin into strips, fry it in oil until crisp, and then use it to garnish each serving of Gravlaks.

CHAPTER TEN
The Three-Hour Cup of Coffee

30 YEARS TOGETHER
It's a love affair that began slowly and continues to grow half a century later. Here Jennifer and I are in Las Vegas in 1997, celebrating the thirtieth anniversary of the day we met on my birthday.

50 YEARS
Shortly after the fiftieth anniversary of the day we met, now in our late seventies, Jennifer and I took our first ride in a Zodiac to see whales at Tofino on Vancouver Island in British Columbia, Canada.

JENNIFER AND LLOYD
Our son Lloyd is a genuinely funny guy, and Jennifer is an easy person to make laugh. Here they are, mugging at our twenty-fifth wedding anniversary lunch at the Los Angeles Music Center, scene of our first date.

JENNIFER AND JOHN
Our sons adore their mother. Here are Jennifer and John at a family Thanksgiving buffet at the home of John and his family in Issaquah, Washington State.

*I*f Marna was the sweet poetry of a youthful romance, then Jennifer is the glorious symphony that enriches my life every day.

For fifty-one years, I've looked at her across thousands of tables as we shared meals at home and at restaurants. We've traveled the globe together, raised two sons together, and shared the laughter and tears of a lifetime. I watch her as she sleeps at night, and sometimes it takes my breath away, even after all these years. I stand there before I climb into bed and I smile at her, feeling the gratitude that encompasses me.

Of all the women I have known, dated, held, caressed, and loved, there is only one I should have married. And fortunately I did. That woman is Jennifer Ann Madge Golder Levine. I cannot imagine having lived my life with anyone else.

It didn't start that way. It began more like a bait-and-switch scheme, one that was the product of my own imagination.

I left home Friday night, May 5, 1967, convinced my sister Myrna had invited me to a surprise party for my twenty-eighth birthday. I didn't believe her when she said it was a *bon-voyage* party for her roommate, Gloria. Myrna and Gloria worked together at a tour-packaging company. Gloria was going to accompany a tour group to Japan. But I knew she had been to Japan several times before. I wasn't buying the *bon-voyage* business. They couldn't fool me. This party was on my birthday and I knew what was up.

On top of that, the party was at an apartment on the same block in Hollywood where Marna lived. It had been nearly two years since Marna and I broke up, but I still held out hope we might get back together. And remember, it was Myrna who introduced me to Marna.

There was no doubt in my mind as I drove to Hollywood: I was walking into a surprise birthday party, Marna was going to be there and my world would be right again.

Wrong on every count. The biggest surprise of the night was that it was not a surprise party for me but an actual *bon-voyage* party for Gloria. In your twenties any excuse for a party is acceptable—even someone's third trip to Japan.

If the lure of possibly seeing Marna and a surprise party for me was the bait, Jennifer turned out to be the switch, and what a happy switch it was—though you never would have known it from the way that night went.

We each spoke exactly one sentence to the other the entire night, and she decided I was a jerk because the first thing I said to her was a one-line joke that misfired. Over the years she learned to shrug off hundreds of similar misfires, even as she laughed easily so many other times.

How did it happen? Why did it work? How did the kid who wrote that high school paper titled "Why the Institution of Marriage is Alien to the Human Spirit" end up married to the same woman for nearly five decades and come to feel he would want to live forever if he could do it with her?

In that high school paper I pointed out that when we are growing up, we are told, "Be your own person" and "Don't feel you have to go along with the crowd."

We also are told settling down, getting married, and raising a family are goals to which we should aspire. Trouble is the two don't mesh. A successful marriage demands compromise, accommodation, and sacrifice—all of which infringe on the notion of being your own person. I still believe those things.

So, how do I square it with the fact that Jennifer and I have made it work? The only answer I have is that it's just pure, dumb luck. That and a good therapist every once in a while and a mutual respect and desire to keep it working.

The institution of marriage is a high-risk gamble. No matter how diligently you work at it, there still is a major dose of luck required if it's going to last—not just last but actually work.

There's a hefty measure of randomness involved in the meeting of any two people in the first place. Ours was no different, except in addition to coming from different backgrounds, we also came from different countries.

It took Jennifer surviving Hitler's bombs in England during the war, then leaving her family behind in London at the age of twenty-two to move to New York and later to Los Angeles, where she landed a job at the same place Myrna worked. It took my family leaving Brooklyn and settling in Los Angeles and Myrna landing a job at the same place Jennifer would later land.

For the several months after our less-than-auspicious meeting, Jennifer and I saw each other frequently when Myrna would bring her to dinners at my parents' house on nights when I was there. I got to know and love her laugh, her independence, and her zest for life. She learned I wasn't a jerk after all and, when I asked her out for the first time nearly three months after we met, she said, "yes."

I had reviewers' tickets to a world premiere of a musical at the Dorothy Chandler Pavilion in the Los Angeles Music Center. It was called *Dumas and Sons,* based on the life of Alexandre Dumas. For decades it remained the worst musical either of us ever had seen. After the show, we stopped at a coffee shop near her apartment. We talked until three o'clock in the morning. I didn't know it at the time, but that three-hour cup of coffee was the first step on what would be the very rewarding road we've traveled together. Of course, I don't remember what we talked about in that coffee shop. I do remember that when I said "good night" at her apartment and headed for home, I felt very, very good for the first time in a long time.

Four and a half months later, we went out again. Two dates in seven and a half months—what can I say? I was busy and still fighting the depression over the loss of Marna. My defenses were solidly in place; I was not ready for any kind of relationship. On our second date, Jennifer and I went to the opening night of the annual Las Posadas festival at Olvera Street in downtown Los Angeles. I'm not much for the Christmas stuff, but I've always been big on the food and music of Mexico. That night Jennifer told me she was going back to England to visit her family before emigrating to Australia.

Aha, I thought, *this is safe. She's leaving*. I liked her but I still wasn't ready for anything even approximating a commitment to a relationship.

After that we were together several nights a week, until she left for England the end of January. The night before New Year's Eve in 1967, we were joined by two other couples for an Ella Fitzgerald show at the Cocoanut Grove night club. After the show, we all went to the bar at Yamashiro, a Japanese restaurant with a wonderful view from its perch in the Hollywood Hills. To this day we go there for dinner several times a year, always sitting by a window, gazing at the carpet of lights that spreads across the Los Angeles basin.

We had our twenty-fifth and fortieth wedding anniversary parties at the Dorothy Chandler Pavilion, the scene of our first date, and we attend the opera there regularly. Whenever we are downtown, near Olvera Street, we stop for a few taquitos at Cielito Lindo and I hum some of the music from the Las Posadas festival. Each of these places remains an important symbol of the life we've had together.

That's how it started for Jennifer and me. She went back to England, but instead of going on to Australia, she came back to L.A. Later, she told me she felt she wanted to see where our relationship was going, that it had been unresolved when she left. She always could go to Australia later, she said.

To understand why it lasted—why we have lasted—would require knowledge of earlier relationships that helped define each of us, my love of cooking and Jennifer not minding doing the dishes, Jennifer developing a love for opera and baseball and me learning to enjoy spending an entire day on the ocean to see just one whale because I was with her. There was the luck of mutual trust in raising children, me developing a tolerance for changing a dirty diaper and Jennifer learning to let the kids have the freedom to roam. There was me giving up cigarettes and Jennifer being willing to live through some very tight financial times while I was switching careers from news reporter to political consultant.

I knew before we got married that Jennifer laughs easily and enthusiastically; she knew I say funny things. But neither of us knew the other liked spinach, or beets, or onions. Those are among the vast number of things two people seldom discuss before committing to a life together.

When two people meet and decide to get married, all they really know of each other is what they have chosen to reveal. The rest is discovered in little moments that come later—moments that can change people in ways that either enhance or destroy relationships.

By the time I met Jennifer, even my parents were convinced I would never get married. Now, it's fifty years, two sons, two daughters-in-law, four grandchildren, two hip replacements, one knee replacement, one quadruple coronary bypass surgery, one bladder cancer surgery, and various other maladies later, and we're going stronger than ever. Clearly, there was nothing head over heels about the way it started. But day by day, event by event it just kept on going and growing and working and getting better.

From my life with Jennifer I came to believe that in a relationship *each* is more important than *both*, and *I* is more important than *we*. *Each* is where the individual exists and it isn't healthy if either individual becomes subjugated to the other and ceases to exist.

As for *we*, that one drives me nuts. "We like this restaurant" or "We liked that movie." Don't they have individual opinions? Has the *we* completely eliminated one or both individuals? I believe this because it's the way Jennifer and I have lived together. Each of us can go off and do something without the other because of a trust that has become instinctive. Jennifer can take off to visit our sons and their families in Northern California or Washington at times when I can't make it. I go to sushi dinners or lunches with friends—mostly women—without Jennifer because she's not big on sushi and because most of my friends are women. Those are things that are important to the *I* in each of us, which in turn strengthens the *we*.

Our doctor said to me once, "You two are really independent."

I answered, "Yes, and yet we are very dependent on each other."

When it works as it has for us, when it works with accommodation that isn't imposed, with compromise that isn't forced, and without the sacrifice that will turn to resentment, there's only one explanation—pure, dumb luck. I've had a large enough share for several people. For that, and for Jennifer, I am incredibly fortunate and deeply thankful.

As for that night in May 1967, it wasn't a surprise birthday party for me, but I got the best birthday present of my life. It was the night I met Jennifer.

If this book were a movie and needed the name of a leading lady above the title on the marquee, that name would be Jennifer. She truly is a beautiful woman—a beautiful person.

Jennifer is a beach person. She loves the ocean. For me it's mountains and trees. We were walking among the giant redwoods in the Sequoia National Forest one morning, when Jennifer said, "So much beauty if you just stop to look at it." That moment, that remark, captures Jennifer more completely and accurately than anything I could say about her.

Jennifer has had a dropped left foot for some time. If she isn't mindful of it, she can trip and fall. So, when we were walking beside the harbor at Boscastle in Cornwall, England, I thought I would need to assist her in climbing some slate and shale steps for a different view of the area. I had been taking photos of the harbor, and when I turned to help Jennifer up the steps, she wasn't where I had last seen her. She had made her way up the steps on her own and was seated on a ledge halfway up the hill. She was smiling as she looked out over the harbor. I climbed to where she sat. "This is the definition of you," I said, "you will not be defeated."

I have cooked for Jennifer more than I have for anyone else. I estimate we've probably eaten at least thirty-seven thousand breakfasts, lunches, and dinners together at home or at restaurants. She enjoys food every bit as much as I do and there is no recipe in this book that wouldn't be appropriate for her. The first recipe in this chapter is for a dish Jennifer makes: Jennifer's Best in the World Meat Loaf. The rest of the recipes are some of Jennifer's favorites, dishes I've created that we enjoy together.

Jennifer's Best in the World Meat Loaf

Early in our married years, before Jennifer went to work outside our home, she regularly cooked dinners for the four of us. We can't recall where she found the original version of this meat loaf recipe. We do know that after making it once, she began to alter and adapt it until it became her own. Her meat loaf is a family legend. Even people who say they don't like meat loaf request this one.

> 2 pounds ground beef, fat content 15% or less
> 1/2 teaspoon salt
> 1/4 teaspoon pepper
> 2 eggs
> 1/2 cup uncooked 1-minute oatmeal
> 1/2 cup milk
> 1/2 cup diced onion
> 1 teaspoon marjoram
> 3/4 cup red wine, divided

Using your hands, thoroughly mix together the first eight ingredients and 1/2 cup of the wine. Form the mixture into a loaf and place it on a lightly greased roasting pan. Pour 1/4 cup of the wine over the loaf. Bake in a preheated oven at 350 degrees for one hour. Remove the loaf to a carving platter, cover the loaf loosely with tinfoil, and let it sit for 10 minutes to seal in juices.

Serve with mashed potatoes.

Makes four to six servings.

Note: You can prepare the loaf ahead of time and refrigerate. Take it out of the refrigerator about one-half our before you plan to put it in the oven.

Shrimp Marsala

Soon after we met, Jennifer told me shrimp was one of her favorite foods. So, I set about the task of developing my own wrinkles on old standards and creating an assortment of shrimp dinners for her.

> 1/2 cup chopped onion
> 2 tablespoons butter
> 1/2 pound sliced mushrooms
> 1 1/2 cups tomato sauce
> 3/4 cup dry Marsala wine
> 1/4 teaspoon each salt, paprika, rosemary
> 1/4 cup half-and-half
> 1 tablespoon cornstarch
> cold water as needed
> 1 pound shelled, cooked shrimp
> 3/4 cup cubed mozzarella cheese
> 4-6 thick slices French bread
> sour cream (optional)
> more paprika, to garnish

In a skillet, lightly sauté the onions in a small amount of the butter. Add the mushrooms and sauté until lightly browned. Remove the onions and mushrooms from the pan.

Combine the tomato sauce, Marsala wine, salt, paprika, rosemary and half-and-half in the pan. Heat to a boil. Mix the cornstarch to a smooth paste with the cold water. Stir the cornstarch into the sauce. Cook and stir until the sauce is smooth and thickened. Add the shrimp, onions and mushrooms.

In the meantime, butter the French bread lightly on both sides, and warm it in a low oven until lightly browned on both sides.

Stir the cheese into the shrimp mixture and pile the shrimp and sauce on the bread. Top each serving with a dollop of sour cream if you like. Sprinkle with some more paprika.

Serves four to six.

Linguine with Shrimp

> 1/4 pound of linguine
> 1 tablespoon of extra-virgin olive oil
> 2 large garlic cloves, finely chopped
> 3 tablespoons shallots, finely chopped
> 2 large tomatoes, coarsely chopped
> 1 tablespoon dried basil, crushed
> 1/4 pound small shrimp, shelled and deveined (not Bay shrimp)
> 2 scallions, chopped
> salt and freshly ground pepper to taste

In a large pot of boiling water, cook the linguine according to package directions. Meanwhile, in a heavy skillet, heat the oil over high heat. Add the garlic and shallots and sauté for about 30 seconds, stirring constantly. Add the tomatoes and basil. Cook for about 1 minute, stirring constantly. Add the shrimp and cook, stirring constantly, until the shrimp are pink and cooked through, about 8 minutes. Sprinkle with scallions and season with salt and pepper to taste. Spoon the shrimp and tomatoes over the hot linguine.

Serve with garlic bread and a small green salad.

Makes two servings.

Scampi

> 1/4 cup butter
> 3 garlic cloves, finely chopped (more or less to taste)
> 1 tablespoon Dry Vermouth
> 1 pound large shrimp, peeled and deveined
> 1/4 teaspoon dried tarragon
> 4 scallions, white and crisp green parts, diced
> 1/4 cup chopped fresh parsley

Melt the butter in a wide frying pan until very hot. Add the garlic and stir for 10 seconds. Add the Vermouth and tarragon and simmer for 1 minute. Add the shrimp and stir to fully coat with butter and garlic. Stir occasionally until the shrimp are pink and cooked through, about 5 to 8 minutes. Add the scallions and stir for about 1 minute. Remove the pan from the heat. Sprinkle parsley over the shrimp.

Remove the shrimp to individual plates and pour the garlic-butter sauce (pan drippings) over the shrimp.

Serve with a small side of pasta tossed in olive oil with garlic. Have some crusty bread available to mop up the garlic butter after you've eaten the shrimp.

Makes two large portions.

Lamb Shoulder Chops

My mother knew only one kind of lamb—broiled shoulder chops. I loved them when she served them for dinner and I still do.

> 1 lamb shoulder chop per person (6 to 8 ounces each)
> lemon juice
> pepper, granulated garlic, and dried rosemary

Put the chops on a rack over a shallow roasting pan. Squeeze fresh lemon juice on each chop. Sprinkle lightly with pepper, granulated garlic and the rosemary that has been crushed in your hand.

Set your broiler on high. Put the chops in the oven, four inches below the broiler heat source, for 4 minutes. Turn the chops. Squeeze on a little more lemon juice and sprinkle on a little more pepper and granulated garlic. Turn the broiler down to medium. Return the chops to the oven and broil another 4 minutes for medium rare.

Serve with sautéed spinach and/or mashed or roasted potatoes.

Leg of Lamb – Four Ways

After a lifetime of eating only lamb shoulder chops, I was introduced to other cuts of lamb by Jennifer and her sister, Sylvia, both British born. Now lamb is my favorite meat; we enjoy it often at home and in restaurants.

1 shank half leg of lamb (4 to 5 pounds)

MARINADES:

French style
1/2 cup white wine
2 garlic cloves, crushed
1 teaspoon tarragon
1/4 cup finely diced onions
1/8 teaspoon freshly ground black pepper

Italian style
1/2 cup red wine
2 garlic cloves, crushed
1 teaspoon oregano
1 teaspoon basil
1/4 cup finely diced onions

Indian style
1/2 cup apple juice
1 garlic clove, crushed
1 tablespoon curry powder (heat to your taste)
1 teaspoon cumin

Middle Eastern style
1/4 cup olive oil
3 tablespoons lemon juice
1 garlic clove, crushed
1 teaspoon oregano
several broken mint leaves
1/2 teaspoon cinnamon
1/4 teaspoon nutmeg

Combine all the ingredients for the marinade you choose. Do it the night before if you can and let it sit overnight to allow the flavors to blend, or do it as early in the day as possible.

Remove the covering skin from the lamb. Pierce the lamb with about 30 jabs of a pointed knife. Place the lamb in a glass or stainless-steel roasting pan. Pour the marinade over the lamb. Turn to coat on all sides. Use your fingers to spread the marinade to places that don't get covered when the lamb is turned. Put the lamb in the refrigerator, uncovered, for at least two hours, the longer the better. Turn the lamb in the marinade occasionally.

About 45 minutes before you plan to start cooking, remove the lamb from the refrigerator. When you are ready to cook, pour off and discard the marinade and place the lamb on a rack in a shallow roasting pan. Preheat the oven to 325 degrees, and cook the lamb for 25 minutes per pound. Let stand about 10 minutes before carving.

This will feed about four people. If you have a bigger crowd, buy a whole leg of lamb and double the amount of marinade.

The best way to carve a leg of lamb is right at the table. It also makes a great show. Just stand the roast upright on the carving tray, hold the bone with a cloth and slice from top to bottom around the bone.

Save the bone for a lamb stock.

Caution: There may be a debate over who gets the very tasty shank. If you want to avoid a fight, cut away the shank before roasting and save it for a lamb shank dinner.

Here's another idea. Buy the whole leg. Have the butcher cut off the shank half for a roast and cube the rest of the meat for lamb stew or lamb kabobs. Ask the butcher for the bone so you can roast it to make stock for the lamb stew.

Note: Left over lamb from the Indian style makes a wonderful curry.

Lamb Shanks

> 2 tablespoons olive oil
> 4 lamb shanks (about 1 pound each)
> 2 garlic cloves, pressed or crushed
> 2 large onions, sliced
> 2 stalks celery, sliced into 1-inch pieces
> 1 1/4 teaspoons each crushed dried thyme and rosemary
> 1 teaspoon salt
> 3/8 teaspoon fresh ground pepper
> 18 ounces no-salt-added tomato sauce
> 3/4 cup dry red wine (or water)
> 3 tablespoons each cornstarch and cold water (optional)

Heat the oil in a 6-quart saucepan over medium-high heat. Add the shanks two at a time, and brown them on all sides. Remove the shanks, add the garlic and onions to the pan and sauté them until they are lightly browned. Return the shanks to the pan. Add the celery, thyme, rosemary, salt, pepper, tomato sauce and wine or water. Bring to a boil, cover, and reduce the heat. Simmer until the meat is tender, about 2 to 2 1/2 hours.

At this point, you may remove the shanks from the pot, allow everything to cool slightly and refrigerate until the next day.

The next day, skim the fat that has congealed at the top of the sauce. If the sauce in the pot is not thick enough, mix together the cornstarch and water. Stir the cornstarch into the hot juices. Cook over medium-high heat, stirring until the sauce thickens. Return the shanks to the sauce and heat through.

I often use my emersion blender to incorporate the vegetables into the sauce after skimming the fat. It gives the sauce more body and a nice flavor.

Note: Most of the time when I make this, I don't need the cornstarch to thicken the sauce.

Serve with white rice, the pan juices, and/or peas, carrots, broccoli, or sautéed spinach.

Serves four.

American Lamb Stew

> 1 tablespoon olive oil
> 1 pound lamb stew meat
> 1 quart lamb stock
> 1 bay leaf (preferably laurel)
> 1/6 cup low-sodium soy sauce
> 1/4 teaspoon freshly ground black pepper
> 2 stalks celery, cut in 1-inch pieces
> 2 large carrots, peeled and cut in 1 inch pieces
> 1 very large brown onion, cut in chunks

Heat the oil in a Dutch oven or a similar vessel. Brown the lamb in the hot oil. Add the stock, bay leaf, soy sauce, and pepper. Bring to a boil. Add the remaining ingredients. Return the pot to a boil. Lower the heat to a slow boil for 1 1/2 hours. Refrigerate for several hours or overnight. Skim off the fat. Bring to a slow boil for 45 minutes.

Serve with some crusty bread.

Serves four.

Irish Stew

On our first night in Ireland Jennifer and I went to Foley's Pub in Dublin for dinner. Irish stew was on the menu and I had to order it to see if it was as good as the one I make at home. I'm happy to report Jennifer and I deemed it a tie. This Irish Stew is every bit as good as what you can get in a pub in Ireland. Too bad the Guinness sold in the States doesn't match what they serve in Ireland. But talk about comfort food. When Jennifer was in the hospital some time ago, I brought helpings of this Irish stew for her dinner. Each night she asked for more of the same the next night.

> 1 1/2 pounds lamb stew meat, cut into 1 1/2-inch cubes
> 3 cups lamb stock, divided
> 3 medium White Rose potatoes
> 3 medium onions
> 3 medium carrots
> 3/4 teaspoon salt
> 1/4 teaspoon pepper

Trim any large chunks of fat from the lamb. Place the meat in a large saucepan with 2 cups of stock. Bring to a boil. Cover and simmer for 1 1/2 hours.

Peel the potatoes, onions and carrots. Cut the vegetables into thick slices. Add the vegetables to the stew pot. Add salt, pepper and 1 more cup of stock. Cover and simmer 45 minutes longer.

Shepherd's Pie

This is another British favorite of which I never heard until Jennifer entered my life. Now, she says mine is as good as or better than any she's ever tasted.

> 3 tablespoons extra-virgin olive oil
> 1 medium onion, diced
> 1 pound ground lamb
> 1/2 cup frozen peas
> 1/2 cup diced carrots
> 1 teaspoon dried rosemary, crushed
> salt and pepper
> 1 large russet potato, cut into quarters lengthwise and then cut into half-inch pieces
> butter, milk, salt, and pepper for the mashed potatoes

Heat the oil in a frying pan. Add the onions and sauté until soft and slightly brown. Add the lamb and break it apart with a wooden spoon. As it browns, continue breaking apart the meat until almost all the pink is gone.

While the lamb is browning, cook the peas as per package directions. Put the carrots in a saucepan with about 1 cup of water. Bring it to a boil for 10 minutes. Drain the peas and carrots.

When the lamb is browned, add the rosemary, peas, and carrots; add the salt and pepper to taste.

In the meantime, bring the potatoes to a boil in enough water to cover. Keep at a moderate boil for 10 minutes. Test the potatoes for doneness with the point of a knife. When the potatoes are done, drain them and mash them with a potato masher.

Add a healthy lump of butter and enough milk to give you a creamy textured mash. Whisk in salt and pepper to taste.

Distribute the lamb mixture into two 1 1/2-cup ramekins. Top each with mashed potatoes. Place in the oven about 4 inches below the broiler heat source. Set the broiler to medium and broil until the top of the potatoes start to take on a nice brown color, about 15 minutes.

Serves two.

Curried Chicken

Another benefit of having a Brit in your life is that you learn about Indian curry. I tasted it for the first time in a long-forgotten restaurant at dinner with Jennifer and I instantly became a fan. From there I learned to love just about all Indian food. While visiting our niece and her family in England some years ago, I cooked the following dish. When I got home and told my friend, Amanda, about it, she exclaimed, "You cooked a curry for a Brit!" Her mother was British; she understood the irony.

> 2 tablespoons olive oil
> 1 onion, halved and sliced
> 1/2 cup water
> 3 tablespoons all-purpose flour
> 1 tablespoon hot curry powder
> 2 tablespoons medium curry powder
> 2 cups fat-skimmed chicken stock, heated
> 2 garlic cloves, chopped
> florets of 1/4 head of cauliflower
> 1 medium carrot, peeled and sliced
> 1/2 cup frozen peas
> 4 chicken thighs, skinless and boneless, cut into bite-size pieces
> 1/4 cup currants
> 1 1/2 teaspoons garam masala

Heat the oil in a wide frying pan. Add the onions, and sauté until soft and lightly browned, stirring to prevent burning. Add the water, cover, and simmer for 15 minutes. Then uncover and continue to simmer until all the water has evaporated.

Add the garlic and sauté lightly. Turn the heat to medium. Stir the flour into the onions and garlic. Cook until flour turns nutty brown (to avoid floury taste), stirring often to prevent burning. Add the curry powder and stir to incorporate with the onions. Add the chicken stock slowly in small amounts, stirring constantly with a wooden spoon to thicken and avoid lumping. As you go, use the spoon to dislodge browned bits from the bottom of the pan. Cover the pan and simmer for 15 minutes.

In the meantime, parboil the cauliflower and carrots, and thaw the peas as per package direction.

Add the chicken and parboiled vegetables; let it simmer until the chicken is cooked through, about 20 minutes. Add the peas and currants and heat through. Remove from the heat and stir in the garam masala.

Serve over white rice.

Serves four.

Lamb Curry

You may notice this dish is called Lamb Curry and the next one is Shrimp Curry, while the previous one is Curried Chicken. It's a cultural thing. The British use the curried first and the type of protein second. On menus in Indian restaurants, it's the opposite. Not wanting anyone to feel slighted, I'm doing it both ways.

> 1/2 cup brown rice*
> 3 tablespoons extra virgin olive oil
> 1 large onion, sliced in half rings
> 3 tablespoons all-purpose flour
> 1 tablespoon hot curry powder
> 2 tablespoons medium curry powder
> 2 garlic cloves, chopped
> 2 cups lamb stock
> 3 cups cooked lamb, cut in cubes from 3/4 inch to 1 inch**
> 1 red-skinned apple, cored, peeled, and sliced
> 1/2 cup currants

Prepare the rice according to package directions.

Heat the oil in a frying pan. Add the onions. Turn the heat up to medium. Toss the onions in the oil to coat; cook until softened and just beginning to brown. Sprinkle the flour over the onions and stir well. Turn the heat down to medium-low and let the flour cook several minutes, until it is a nutty brown color. Stir frequently to avoid burning and assure all the flour is cooked. Add the curry powder and garlic, and stir them with the onions. Let the curry powder cook for about one minute.

Slowly add about 2 cups of lamb stock, a little at a time, stirring constantly to incorporate the flour and thicken the sauce. When the sauce comes to a very slow boil, turn the heat down, cover the pan, and maintain at simmer for 15 minutes. Stir occasionally to prevent the mixture from sticking to the pan and burning. Add more broth or water if the mixture becomes too thick.

Add the lamb and apple to the sauce. Cover and let everything heat through. Add the currants to heat and plump them.

Mound the rice in the middle of two plates. Spoon the lamb and curry sauce over the rice and serve.

Use long-grain white rice if you prefer.
Leftover lamb from a French or Italian-style leg of lamb works well for this.

Serves two.

Shrimp Curry

> 1/2 cup brown rice
> 10 large raw shrimp, shell on
> 2 1/2 cups of water
> 1/2 large brown onion
> 3 tablespoons of olive oil
> 3 tablespoons all-purpose flour
> 1 tablespoon hot curry powder
> 2 tablespoons medium curry powder
> 2 garlic cloves, crushed
> 1/4 cup golden raisins

Cook the rice according to package directions.

Peel the shrimp and remove the tails. Put the shells and tails in a saucepan with the water. Cover and bring to a boil. Turn the heat down to maintain at a slow boil for 20 minutes. Strain the broth into a measuring cup and discard the shells.

Slice the onion into rings about 1/8 inch thick; then cut the rings in half. Heat the oil in a frying pan. Add the onions. Turn the heat up to medium. Stir the onions to coat them in the oil. Sauté the onions until they are softened and just beginning to brown, stirring frequently. Sprinkle the flour over the onions and stir well to distribute. Turn the heat down to medium-low and let the flour cook several minutes until it is a nutty brown color. Stir frequently to cook evenly and avoid burning. Add the curry powder and garlic and stir with the onions. Let the curry powder cook for about one minute. Then slowly add 2 cups of the shrimp broth in small batches, stirring constantly to incorporate the flour and thicken the sauce. When the sauce comes to a very slow boil, turn the heat down, cover the pan, and maintain it at a simmer for 15 minutes. Stir occasionally to prevent the mixture from sticking to the pan. Add more shrimp broth or water if the mixture turns too thick.

Add the shrimp and raisins, stir well, bring the sauce back to a simmer, cover and cook for 4 minutes. Stir the mixture again, cover, and cook another 4 minutes. When the shrimp look done all the way through, remove the pan from the heat.

Mound the rice in the middle of two plates. Spoon the shrimp and curry sauce over the rice.

Serves two.

Pot Roast with Vegetables

> 1 chuck roast, about 3 pounds
> 2 tablespoons vegetable oil
> 1 large onion, sliced
> 2 cups water, as needed, divided
> 1 teaspoon salt
> 1/4 teaspoon black pepper
> 2 carrots, peeled and cut into 1-inch pieces (more if desired)
> 1 large russet potato, peeled and cut into bite-size pieces (more if desired)

Trim the fat from the roast. Divide the meat along the natural lines.

Heat the oil in a large frying pan. Sauté the onions in the oil until they begin to brown. Remove the onions from the pan. Sear both sides of the meat in the hot oil. Remove the meat from the pan.

Add 1/2 cup of the water to the pan to deglaze. Scrape the bottom of the pan with a spatula to free any stuck bits. Bring the water to a boil, and then turn the heat down to low.

Return the meat to the pan. Layer the onions on top of the meat. Add another 1/2 cup of water. Bring to a boil. Cover the pan and cook over low heat for 2 hours. Check occasionally to be sure some liquid remains and the meat isn't sticking to the bottom of pan. Add more water as needed, about 1/2 cup at a time.

Add one cup of water and bring it to a boil. Add the carrots and potatoes to the pan beside the meat. Cover and cook for

1/2 hour at a moderate boil. Test the potato for doneness with the point of a knife. The roast is ready when potatoes are done.

Serves four large portions. If there is any left over, just reheat it with a little water in the pan the next night.

This recipe can easily be scaled up to a larger roast if you have a large enough pan. You also could use a Dutch oven.

Seafood Filé Gumbo

> 1/2 pound large raw shrimp, shell on
> 2 cups of water
> 1 1/2 cups chicken broth, divided
> 1 cup long-grain white rice
> 1 cup coarsely chopped onions
> 2 tablespoons olive oil
> 1 can (14 1/2-ounce) stewed tomatoes, coarsely chopped
> 3 medium mushrooms, sliced
> 8 okra, sliced into approximately 1/4-inch rings
> 2 large garlic cloves, finely chopped
> 1/4 teaspoon cayenne powder (or less), to taste
> 1/2 teaspoon each paprika and dried tarragon
> 1 teaspoon dried oregano, crushed
> 1 teaspoon dried basil, crushed
> 4-5 drops Tabasco sauce, to taste
> 1 1/4 pounds fleshy white fish (rock fish, orange roughy, cod, sea bass—not Chilean) cut into bite-size pieces
> 1 1/2 teaspoons filé gumbo (powdered)

Peel and devein the shrimp. Set the shrimp aside. Put the shrimp shells and tails in a small saucepan. Add 2 cups of water. Bring to a boil. Reduce the heat and boil slowly for 20 minutes. Pour the liquid through a strainer into a measuring cup. Discard the shells.

Put 1 cup of the chicken broth and all of the shrimp stock in a 4-quart saucepan, and bring to a low boil. Add the rice, stir gently, cover, and cook 15 minutes.

While the rice is cooking, sauté the onions in about 2 tablespoons of oil in a wide frying pan. Remove the pan from the heat when the onions are lightly browned.

Put the tomatoes, mushrooms, okra, garlic, cayenne powder, paprika, tarragon, oregano, basil and Tabasco in a glass or stainless steel bowl and mix them together.

When the rice is done, add it to the pan with the sautéed onions. Add the vegetable mixture and the remaining 1/2 cup of chicken broth. Stir together thoroughly, cover, and boil slowly for about 20 minutes, until the okra is softened. Add the fish and shrimp and cook at a slow boil for 5 minutes. If the shrimp is not yet fully opaque, cook for an additional minute or two, until the shrimp is cooked through.

Ladle the gumbo into individual bowls and sprinkle filé gumbo on top of each bowl.

Serve with crusty French bread.

Serves four.

Think-Thin Paella

This is the first thing I cooked for my future daughter-in-law, Edie. At the time, I still was being fanatical about my post-coronary-bypass surgery diet. I did it all on the stove top because I didn't have a proper Paella pan. Now that time has passed and I'm a bit looser with my diet, I fry up some chorizo and add it to this dish at the last step.

1 cup of fat-skimmed chicken stock
1/4 cup dry white wine
1 teaspoon dried basil, crushed
1 teaspoon dried tarragon, crushed
1/2 teaspoon garlic salt
1 chicken breast, skinned, boned, and cut into 1-inch pieces
4 large chicken thighs, skinned
salt and pepper
1 teaspoon dried oregano, crushed
3 tablespoons olive oil
1 medium onion, halved and sliced thin
1 garlic clove, finely chopped
3/4 cup long-grain white rice
1 1/2 cups water
1/2 teaspoon paprika
1 teaspoon dried thyme, crushed
pinch powdered saffron *or* 4 saffron threads
dash Tabasco sauce
1/8 teaspoon chili powder
1 cup crushed tomatoes (if canned, drain off most of the liquid) *or* 1 cup fresh tomatoes, peeled, seeded, and chopped
2 dozen large shrimp (50–70 count size), peeled and deveined
1 cup frozen peas
1/4 pound ham steak, finely diced

Mix the chicken stock, white wine, basil, tarragon and garlic salt in a saucepan. Bring it to a boil. Add the chicken breast pieces. Return to a slow boil and poach the chicken 5 minutes. Remove the chicken from the liquid and set it aside.

Coat the chicken thighs with oil and sprinkle them with salt, pepper and oregano. Place the thighs on a baking sheet and bake in preheated oven at 350 degrees for 40 minutes, turning once.

Heat the oil in a 12-inch fry pan. Add the onion and sauté until it is softened but not browned. Add the garlic and rice and shake the pan to coat the rice with oil. Add the water, paprika, thyme, saffron, Tabasco and chili powder. Stir the ingredients in the pan to mix well. Cover and bring to a simmer for 15 minutes. Add the tomatoes, shrimp, peas, ham and chicken breast pieces. Stir well. (Add 1/8 cup of water if the rice is overly dry.) Place the chicken thighs on top of the mixture. Cover. Increase the heat slightly and cook until the shrimp are pink all the way through, the peas and chicken are heated through, and all the water has evaporated, about 7 to 8 minutes. Tilt the pan lid to allow the moisture to escape if any water remains.

Spoon the paella onto individual plates. Be sure each plate contains 3 shrimp and one chicken thigh or leg. Serve with a small green salad with mild vinaigrette or Italian dressing and crusty French bread.

Makes four generous portions.

Chicken with Black Beans and Rice

> 2 chicken thighs — bone in, skinless
> 1 tablespoon olive oil
> 1 teaspoon cumin
> 1 (15-ounce) can no-salt-added black beans (or prepare them yourself from dried beans)
> 1/2 cup uncooked flavorful rice medley*
> 1 cup water
> 3/4 tablespoon Creole or Santa Fe spice mixture
> 1/2 onion, coarsely diced
> 1 large tomato, diced

Preheat the oven to 400 degrees. Coat the chicken with olive oil. Rub the cumin onto both sides of the chicken. Put the chicken on a rack over a shallow roasting pan, and bake for 10 minutes. Turn the chicken over and bake for 10 more minutes. I find the chicken cooks better and tastes better if you leave the bone in.

Heat the black beans in a saucepan.

Cook the rice in another saucepan according to package directions.

Stir the spice mixture into the beans. Mix the cooked rice into the beans. Add the raw onion to the beans and rice.

To serve, center the chicken on a plate, spoon the rice and beans mixture over the chicken, and top with the diced tomato.

For the rice, I like something called RiceSelect Royal Blend by Rice Tec Inc. It's a mixture of Texmati white, brown, wild, and red rice. Anything along the same lines probably would work as well.

Serves two.

Chicken in Mushroom Sauce

> 1 package (1/2 ounce) dried porcini or morel mushrooms
> 2 1/2 cups very hot tap water
> 2 tablespoons olive oil
> 1/2 large onion, cut into half moons
> water
> 3 tablespoons all-purpose flour
> 1 teaspoon dried fines herbs, crushed
> salt and pepper to taste
> 2 large skinless, bone-in chicken thighs

Soak the mushrooms in the hot water in a covered saucepan for 30 minutes. Drain the mushrooms through a strainer, reserving the liquid in a measuring cup. Thoroughly rinse the mushrooms in hot water to remove any remaining grit. Cut the mushrooms into small pieces. If you are using morels be sure to slice them lengthwise first, and then rinse the mushrooms again in hot water.

In the meantime, heat the oil in a wide frying pan. Add the onions and sauté until they start to brown. Add 1/2 cup of water, cover, and let the onions stew for 15 minutes. Check to be sure there is still some liquid in the pan so the onions don't burn. Remove the cover and continue to sauté until the liquid is gone.

Sprinkle the flour through a fine strainer onto the onions. Stir to evenly distribute the flour. Cook, uncovered, over medium-low heat until the flour is nutty brown, stirring frequently to assure the flour is cooked evenly and does not burn.

Slowly add the mushroom water to the pan, stirring constantly. Use a wooden spoon to stir and scrape the browned bits from the bottom of the pan. Continue to slowly add more water and stir to thicken, until you have used almost all the mushroom water. Leave some of the water at the bottom of the measuring cup so you don't accidently pour grit into the sauce.

When all the water has been stirred into the onions, add the fines herbs, salt and pepper. Stir, cover, and simmer for 15 minutes.

Add the chicken thighs, turning to coat both sides. Cover and cook at a moderate boil for 10 minutes. Turn the thighs and boil for another 10 minutes.

Plate the thighs and spoon the mushroom sauce over them.

I serve this only with mashed potatoes, which I also bathe in a healthy helping of the mushroom sauce.

Serves two.

Oh, Those Golden Pork Chops

> 2 tablespoons olive oil
> 1/2 medium onion, sliced thin
> 1 yellow bell pepper, seeded and sliced
> 1 teaspoon medium-hot curry powder
> 1/2 tablespoon all-purpose flour
> 1/2 cup chicken broth
> 1 tablespoon whole-grain or stoneground mustard
> 2/3 cup dried apricots, cut in halves

Heat the oil in a wide frying pan. Add the onion and bell pepper, and stir over medium heat for about 5 minutes. Stir in the curry powder and flour and cook until the flour is browned and loses its raw flour taste, about 10 minutes. Add the chicken broth slowly, stirring to thicken. Stir in the mustard and apricots. Raise the heat to medium and put the pork chops in the pan. Cover and cook for about 6 minutes. Turn the pork chops over, cover again, and cook for another 6 minutes.

Note: If the pork chops are less than 3/4 inch thick, reduce the cooking time to 4 minutes per side.

To serve, put a pork chop on each plate. Top it with the onions, bell peppers and apricots. This goes well with rice or with boiled white potatoes.

CHAPTER ELEVEN
An Indomitable Spirit, An Incredible Survival

SISTERS
My mother (Chapter 1), right, with her younger sister Tillie Tooter. My beloved Aunt Tillie came west to be at the luncheon celebrating Jennifer's and my twenty-fifth wedding anniversary.

TILLIE'S KITCHEN
We visited Tillie often at her home in Florida. Tillie and Jennifer quickly formed a loving bond. This photo of me with Tillie was snapped in her kitchen in Pembroke Pines, Florida.

We sat at the small table in the tiny dining area of the cramped kitchen in a downstairs South Florida condo, part of a complex that was home to thousands of Jewish transplants from the chilled winters of New York and New Jersey. It was Jennifer, Aunt Tillie and me.

Outside, the temperature and humidity were climbing steadily, even that early in the morning. The dishes from our lox and bagel breakfast had been cleared. I was on my third cup of coffee. Jennifer had quit after one and Tillie drank just water.

Tillie Tooter was my mother's younger sister. If you walk into our house, you'll see Tillie and Mom smiling broadly in a photograph in our entry hall.

Until that morning in Tillie's kitchen the enormity of what happened to her was an abstraction—something we read about in the newspaper, saw on TV, and discussed on the telephone. Now, I was looking into the face of this remarkable woman, who had been part of my life since the moment I was born.

For eighty-three years Tillie Tooter lived her life in quiet anonymity. A World War II widow, she raised her daughter alone in the years before society coined the term *single mom*. Then, in the predawn darkness on a South Florida highway in the summer of 2000, her anonymity was ripped away by a drunk driver who rammed her car from behind and sent her careening over the guardrail of a bridge into the mangroves forty feet below. He didn't stop.

As police searched for Tillie for three agonizing days, she became an international celebrity, whose fame would last a lot longer than the proverbial fifteen minutes.

For years after that near-fatal night, you could go anywhere in South Florida with Tillie and expect people to approach her. "You're Tillie, aren't you," they would say, or "Tillie, you're such an inspiration. How are you?"

Newspaper headlines at the time called her "Swamp Granny" and "Tough Tillie." We laughed at the imagery. Tillie was not the frail, eighty-three-year-old grandmother people might have imagined from the news stories. Her mind remained sharp, she played poker several times a week, and she had control of her faculties well into her nineties. She didn't stop driving until she was ninety-seven, and there was no reason why she should have stopped sooner. As a result of the accident, however, she needed a walker or a wheelchair to navigate long distances and her torn rotator cuff never recovered.

Tillie's life had been heroic long before that fateful night. Like so many others, she had known life's sorrows. Her first husband, Irving Zucker, was the uncle who accompanied me and my father to my first baseball game at Ebbets Field in Brooklyn. Then he shipped out and was killed during the Allied liberation of France two months later. At the age of twenty-eight Tillie was left alone to raise her only child, my cousin Linda.

Tillie knew her share of joys too, starting with her adored daughter and two grandchildren, Eric and Lori. Then there was her sister, Norma (my mother), a son-in-law, a few of us nephews around the country, who remained close to her, and a circle of friends everywhere she went. And there were three great-granddaughters. The twins called her "GG"—for Great-Grandma.

I was not quite four years old when Tillie gave birth to

Linda. I was so crazy about my new little cousin that when my youngest sister was born soon after, I insisted she be named Linda. My parents went along for a short time. Then they decided they really wanted her to be named after my mother's mother and they changed her name from Linda to Elisa.

That should give you some idea of how I felt about my aunt Tillie at a very early age. One of the more difficult things about moving from Brooklyn to Los Angeles was leaving Tillie behind. She had a big, loving, welcoming spirit and a hearty laugh that made you want to be with her.

Tillie would marry twice more. The second marriage didn't work. The third one did—big time. She and Ed Tooter were the definition of devotion, love and respect until he died, once again leaving Tillie a widow.

Some aunts and uncles are wonderful with young nephews and nieces but don't know how to relate to them as adults. Not Tillie. As a kid, I looked forward to being in the circle of her love. In Brooklyn we lived just a few blocks from her and Linda. On many summer days we would walk through Lincoln Terrace Park to visit them at their apartment. Sometimes they would meet us—my mother, my two sisters and me—at Betsy Head Park, where we would spend hot, humid summer days splashing in the wading pool.

In later years I always knew Tillie would greet me not just as her sister's son but as an adult member of her family. Before she moved to Florida, I considered time with Tillie a must whenever I visited New York. After she moved, Jennifer and I made trips to Florida primarily to visit her, sometimes for a birthday celebration and sometimes just to be there.

I first learned Tillie was missing after the accident in 2000 when we got a phone call from my mother. Jennifer and I had been on vacation in Northern California for a week. We were home just a few minutes when the phone rang. Through tears, Mom said, "Tillie died." Mom told me she received a call from a friend who lived in L.A. and heard the news from a mutual friend who heard the news on a Florida television broadcast. I didn't believe it. If Tillie was dead we would have heard from Linda, or my late cousin Irwin, who lived in the same Century Village complex where Tillie lived. We would not have had to learn third-hand through Mom's old friend.

I called Irwin and asked, "What's going on?"

"How do you know anything is going on?" he asked back.

I told him about the chain of phone calls and asked again what was going on.

He told me Tillie had been heading for Hollywood/Fort Lauderdale Airport to pick up her granddaughter Lori and Lori's boyfriend, who were coming from New Jersey for a visit. The plane was late, and Lori called to say she would rent a car or take a cab to Tillie's apartment. Tillie insisted on picking them up. Videotapes of the Century Village exit gate showed her leaving for the airport at 2:54 a.m. She never got there.

Irwin said the family decided not to alarm anyone until they had more information, but it was too late. By the time I spoke with him the story of Tillie's disappearance was being shown on television news programs as far away as London and Australia. Soon we were receiving calls from our relatives in those places, asking what was happening.

Our calls to Florida throughout the next day brought only speculation. We were told police had searched the roadside between Tillie's apartment and the airport and could find no sign of her. They were continuing to search, even using helicopters. Some family members thought she might be the victim of a carjacking or some other form of violence. Police speculated she might have fallen asleep at the wheel at that early hour of the morning or become confused in the darkness around the airport and wandered off.

I never bought any of that. It was the wrong time of day and the wrong place for a carjacking. Carjackers and muggers don't lie in wait near closed airports for people in five-year-old Toyotas at three o'clock in the morning. As for falling asleep,

Tillie was a night person. Her poker games often started at ten o'clock at night. She was going to the airport to pick up her granddaughter. Her adrenaline would have been flowing too fast for her to fall asleep. And disoriented? Absurd. Tillie didn't get disoriented, as her survival story ultimately demonstrated.

From the start, I assumed there had been an accident. Maybe it was the result of a heart attack, stroke, or mechanical failure. It might have involved another car—maybe a drunk driver at that hour of the morning. But the route from her home to the airport was simple and direct. Why weren't they finding her car? For three anxious days we feared the worst and hoped for the best. As the hours passed, my frustration turned to anger, until finally I resolved to fly to Florida and walk the route to the airport. "She's there somewhere, and they're just not finding her," I said.

We went to bed Monday night clinging to a thread of hope, not wanting to admit what we knew was possible. Then, Tuesday morning, while I was getting ready to go to the office, still thinking I would get on a plane and head for Florida, we got a call from my cousin Bob in Los Angeles, another of Tillie's nephews. Tillie had been found; she was alive. Rescue crews were working to free her at that very moment: it was being shown live on national TV.

The story of Tillie's survival and rescue flashed across the nation and around the world. Newspapers and television stations told the story, and the nation fell in love with her—an eighty-three-year-old, red-haired grandmother who survived three days trapped in her car nestled among mangroves just inches above a Florida swamp.

The *New York Post* announced: "Swamp Granny Survives Ordeal." Countless newspapers attached the word *feisty* to her. A cartoonist dubbed her "America's Favorite Grandma." She appeared on *The Early Show* on CBS and the *Today* show on NBC. CNN provided running coverage of her recovery. She was a guest on *Late Show with David Letterman*, and *People* magazine told her story in a two-page spread. The media followed her recovery in the intensive care unit at Broward Medical Center; they covered her homecoming after she was released from the hospital; they ran features on the thousands of cards, letters, flowers and gifts she was receiving from across the nation—including a new Toyota provided by a local dealer to replace the one lost in the collision. On Thanksgiving Day she appeared again on NBC's *Today* show.

Tillie's battle to survive during the seventy-nine hours she was trapped in that car is a marvel. When it rained, she reached out the car window and caught water in an aluminum steering-wheel cover. Then she used a golf sock to absorb the water, which she sucked from the sock to fight off dehydration. I wondered why she had a golf sock in the car—she never played golf. She told us she used it to protect the gearshift stick from the hot sun.

She tore her single stick of gum into five pieces to conserve it, so she could keep moisture in her mouth. When the gum was gone and her only sucking candy used up, she sucked on a button torn from her blouse to create saliva, a trick she said she learned from some long-forgotten western movie. She sang songs from the 1930s and 1940s to keep her mind active. She blew the car horn to try to attract the attention of motorists passing by on a bridge forty feet above. At night, she turned her headlights on in the hope that someone would see them. Then the battery died.

The first report we heard of her rescue said she was alive, alert and able to tell rescue workers her phone number and the number of the flight she was going to meet at the airport.

Later we learned the improbable circumstances that led to her rescue. A fifteen-year-old boy found her while working with his father on a highway cleanup project. He noticed scrapings on a bridge railing and looked over the edge. He saw a car suspended in the mangroves below, and he saw movement inside the car. Tillie had sensed something, stuck her leg out a broken window and wiggled her foot. The boy's father called 911 emergency services.

Tillie's first words to rescue workers were, "Can one of you guys get me out of here?" As they were lifting her from the car to the bridge above, she asked, "Will someone please get my pocketbook?" She was covered from head to toe with insect bites. Her body was battered and bruised.

In conversations with police and interviews with reporters over the next few days, Tillie revealed what happened. As she neared the airport, her car was rear-ended and sent over the guard rail. There she played out her solo drama of hope, and survival with her indomitable spirit.

The ex-journalist in me has wondered what it was about this story that caught the eyes of so many news editors so quickly. I understand why the rescue and survival became a story. It's irresistible human interest. But I would have expected jaded editors to shrug off the original news of her disappearance as a *disoriented old lady who got lost*. News editors tend to be cynics, and they certainly are hardened. The disappearance of *one old lady* in South Florida would not ordinarily catch their interest. For some reason, though, this one did. Whatever the reason, their journalistic instincts proved correct.

As I wrote the first draft of this chapter, I had just returned from another visit to South Florida to see Tillie. My first day in town, I arrived at her apartment at nine in the morning for breakfast. Twelve hours later we were still in the apartment, talking of family, life, love, personal philosophies and just about anything else one could imagine.

One of the funniest things Tillie said about the whole ordeal was, "You know, if my name was Sarah Smith instead of Tillie Tooter no one would have paid any attention. It's the name that did it."

I have kept a selection of memorabilia regarding Tillie's

survival. There are a couple issues of *People* magazine, with full-color photos of Tillie, Linda and Lori. But my favorite is a copy of the South Florida *Sun-Sentinel* with a headline over a story about Tillie's ninetieth birthday party. It reads: "Tillie Tooter at 90: 'I like living'".

On August 1, 2015, the effects of old age did what a drunk driver in a three-thousand-pound steel projectile couldn't do. Tillie Tooter—Aunt Tillie, "Tough Tillie," the "Swamp Granny"—the woman who liked living at least as much as anyone I've ever known, who brought love and laughter and inspiration to so many, died quietly in hospice care in South Florida at the age of 99.

Some people seek glory and never achieve it. Others achieve it and wear the mantle without grace. Still others have it thrust upon them and assume it with inspirational dignity. That was Tillie. Her inspiring life and survival made her a popular speaker at senior citizen facilities throughout South Florida.

For years, each time I visited Tillie she made the same dinner my first night in town. It started with chopped liver and rye bread. Then there was one of my very favorites: chicken livers with mushrooms, onions and sweetbreads. Finally, she brought out baked brisket of beef. It was more food than anyone should eat at one time and loaded with cholesterol from start to finish. I have my own versions of these dishes. My chopped-liver recipe and my recipe for chicken livers with mushrooms, onions and sweetbreads are very much like Tillie's. My mother prepared them the same way. The brisket recipe, however, is my own creation.

Chopped Liver Appetizer (á la Tillie Tooter)

> 2 tablespoons olive oil, butter, or schmaltz (rendered chicken fat)
> 1 medium onion, sliced thinly and cut into half moons
> 1/2 pound chicken livers
> salt to taste

Heat the butter, oil or schmaltz in a wide frying pan. Sauté the onions until they are soft. Add the livers. Sprinkle the livers lightly with salt. Cover and cook until done, about 15 minutes, stirring occasionally to turn the livers over. Put the livers and onions through a food mill to mash. Add salt to taste; add oil or schmaltz for a smooth texture if the liver is too dry.

Tillie served this with seeded Jewish rye bread as an appetizer. It also serves well with saltine or water crackers.

Tillie's Chicken Livers with Mushrooms, Onions and Sweetbreads

> 3 tablespoons olive oil
> 1 large onion, cut in half and sliced into half moons
> 1/2 cup water
> 1/2 pound sliced mushrooms
> 1/2 pound chicken livers
> 1/4 pound sweetbreads, cut into bite-size pieces*
> 1 cup frozen peas
> salt to taste

Heat the oil over a medium-high flame in a large frying pan. Add the onion, and stir until slightly browned. Add the water, reduce the heat to low, cover and stew until the onions are well browned. Add more water if needed, 1/4 cup at a time, to keep the onions from burning. You want them soft, brown, and sweet.

Return the heat to medium-high, add the mushrooms to the onions, and sauté, stirring occasionally, until the mushrooms are browned. Reduce the heat to medium. Add the chicken livers and stir together with the onions and mushrooms. Cover and stew the livers in their juices for 10 minutes. Add the sweetbreads. Stir all the contents of the frying pan together. Cover and stew the mixture 5 minutes more. Stir in the peas. Cover and let cook at low heat about 5 minutes more. Check to see if the peas are cooked and the sweetbreads are cooked through. Sprinkle on salt to taste.

Serves well over steamed white rice, with pan juices as a sauce.

Serves two.

If I can't find any sweetbreads in a local market, I make this dish without them.

Larry's Baked Brisket of Beef

> 1 brisket of beef, preferably the point end (about 5 pounds)
> 2 tablespoons olive oil
> 2 brown onions, sliced
> paprika
> 2 carrots, sliced
> 2 celery stalks, with leaves, diced
> 1 cup water
> 1 cup red wine

Trim some of the surface fat from the meat, but leave a thin fat crown. Heat the oil in a large frying pan. Sear the brisket on all sides in the hot oil. Transfer the brisket to a roasting pan with a tight cover.

Slightly brown the onion slices in the brisket juices left in the frying pan. (Add more olive oil if needed.)

Sprinkle the brisket generously with paprika. Cover the brisket with the onions. Surround the brisket with the carrots and celery. Add the water and wine along the sides to avoid washing the paprika from the meat. Cover the roasting pan tightly and bake the brisket in a preheated oven at 325 degrees for 2 1/2 hours. Transfer the brisket to a carving platter, cover the meat loosely with tinfoil, and let it stand 10 to 15 minutes so juices can set. Do not remove the onions. With a sharp knife, slice the beef across the grain.

Hint: If the cover of your roasting pan doesn't fit tightly, it's a good idea to check the pan every 45 minutes or so to make sure the liquid hasn't cooked away. Add more water if needed. Or you can seal the top of the pan with tinfoil to form a seal and then place the cover over the foil.

I like to wrap the brisket in tinfoil after it is cooked. Then I put it in the refrigerator overnight and slice it the next day. It slices more easily after it has cooled. After slicing it, I wrap it in tinfoil again. When I'm getting close to serving time, I reheat the brisket in a 325-degree oven. It will take about 30–40 minutes to heat through. Loosen the tinfoil the last 15 minutes. By doing this, you will avoid a last-minute rush of carving the meat. You just need to unwrap the meat and put it on a serving platter.

For a nice gravy, discard the solids from the roasting pan, refrigerate the cooking liquid overrnight, then skim the fat. Heat the liquid to a slow boil, stir in some red wine, salt and pepper to taste, and perhaps add some demi-glace or a lump of butter. Then thicken the gravy slightly with cornstarch.

Serves well with mashed or roasted potatoes and green beans.

Serves six to eight people.

CHAPTER TWELVE

Immortality Is a Granddaughter

ELLA
Jennifer and I were in Italy four months after Ella was born. I sent a postcard addressed to Ella Bella. I still call her that today, my beautiful Ella. This photo was taken at Grandparents' Day at her school.

ALISE
Alise was in the garden, helping her mother plant some flowers at their home, when I stopped by for a visit. The memory of her teaching me yoga on the kitchen floor when she was four years old still makes us laugh—at me, not her.

CARLIE
Carlie is the youngest of our three granddaughters. One day she said, "I'm a big girl." From the next room, it sounded to me like she said, "I'm a bagel." I went rushing over and asked, "Did you say you're a bagel?" Hours later, she was still laughing every time I said, "Hi, bagel."

"The girls" have always known they can count on Jennifer to read and play games with them. In these photos, she's reading to Alise and Carlie and doing a word-search puzzle with Ella. She taught Ella how to play patience (solitaire), and Alise and Carlie love to help when Jennifer gets out the deck of cards.

JENNIFER WITH ELLA

JENNIFER WITH ALISE

JENNIFER WITH CARLIE

ELLA
What a thrill to sit in the third row of the theater and see our Ella sing, dance, and act in a musical production and to watch her mature into a high school student.

ALISE
Alise helped our son Lloyd prepare a baked brisket of beef for a dinner party. But she didn't want to taste the finished product.

CARLIE
Carlie waits anxiously to be served finger sandwiches and cookies that her mom prepared for a special afternoon tea at home.

The calendar said the days of summer were dwindling, but it was Southern California, where we insist there are only two seasons—summer and almost summer. The temperature had edged into the eighties on a mid-September morning. My kind of day—top down on the car, no jacket needed, the *Opera Show* on our local NPR affiliate, not a cloud in sight.

Soprano Anna Netrebko was singing "Sempre Libre" from *La Traviata* as I pulled onto our new paver-stone driveway. I turned off the engine, laid my head back and gazed into the bluest of clear-blue skies. *I'm looking at infinity*, I thought. *There's no end to what I'm seeing. Or hearing.*

If there's any poetry in your soul, there are times when you think things like that. *This music has transcended generations; this voice will be heard through all time. I am at the crossroads of yesterday and tomorrow. And there is nothing in the sky to block my view of infinity.*

When we're young, we think we're immortal, nothing can harm us. Just follow a teenage driver a few blocks through traffic and you'll see what I mean. Or watch the twenty-something guys downing beers at a baseball or football stadium before they hit the road for a bar or club later that night.

When we get older, it dawns on us: we are not immortal after all and we begin to look for links between our recognized mortality and our faded sense of indestructability. Nothing

I have experienced sharpens that focus as keenly as grandchildren. They are the bridges that connect the stories of our family histories to our hopes for the future, the line that runs from our grandparents and parents, through us to all who will come after. Those grandparents who left generations behind to immigrate to a better life, who brought our parents into the world—they are the antecedents; we are the commas in the continuum of life. Our grandchildren are the beginnings of our next chapters.

The first time I saw my first grandchild was in a photo emailed from Kirkland, Washington, by our son John. Ella was just hours old, wrapped in swaddling, lying on her stomach, her head turned to the camera and her eyes wide open.

My first reaction—my first words: "Oh, my god. She's beautiful." Everyone in our suite of offices rushed to see. Of course all grandparents believe their grandchildren are beautiful. But in this case it was true, as evidenced as Ella grew older.

I met all four of our grandchildren the same way, via emailed photos. Two years after Ella was born, John sent the first photo of her brother, Miles. Four years later Lloyd emailed a photo of Alise from Sacramento. Three years after that there was the photo of Alise's little sister Carlie.

Now, you may be wondering what Miles is doing in a book about women. The answer: I couldn't leave him out just because he was born male. He's one of my grandchildren. I love him. I wouldn't want to hurt his feelings. So, Miles, welcome to my world of beautiful women. It's a world that now includes two beautiful and intelligent daughters-in-law and three lovely and smart granddaughters. Miles, I hope your life can be filled with the company of as many wonderful women as I have known.

I could tell stories to illustrate how cute and smart each of the grandchildren is. But that would be no less boring than all the stories told by other proud grandparents of grandchildren we don't know. So instead, let me tell you of my aspirations when I think of our grandchildren.

I want to sit next to them at an opera and give them a chance to sample the art that was handed to me by my mother and grandfather and has thrilled me all through my life. I want to have meaningful discussions with them about society's ills and how to right them. I want to tell them stories of how my parents shaped my life and I want to pass along an awareness of justice and equality and the need to rail against injustice and inequality. I want to see them care about the world in which they live and I want to hear their dreams and ambitions.

I want to take them places and show them things, to travel with them across our nation and abroad as they discover the beauty of our national parks, the thrill of New York City, the allure of Paris, the beauty of Italy. I want to be there the first time they see the Mona Lisa and the statue of David. I want to continue to be silly with them and laugh with them. I want to sit with them in great restaurants, drinking fine wine as we have the kinds of talks in which they can get to know me as adults and I can watch them grow.

I want to stand strong against the years and stay vital enough to do these things and I want them to be able to make memories with their grandfather that will warm them always and be passed on to their children. If I can do that, then the circle will be complete and we will have achieved an infinity as clear as an endless blue sky.

Grandchildren can make you think of yourself as old. Any time Ella or Miles call, "Granddad" or Alise or Carlie say "Grandpa," I want to look around for some old guy. It took some time to get used to the fact that they were talking about me.

At the same time, grandchildren can keep you young. It's been four decades since I sang "Itsy Bitsy Spider" or "The Wheels on the Bus Go Round and Round" to my own children. Now I get to do it again, and I remember the words. Old guys don't remember words after forty years. They forget things after forty minutes.

It's too early to know if and how their tastes for food will develop. At young ages, their interests have varied widely and changed frequently.

Ella is a pescatarian, as is her mother. She particularly enjoys good salmon, which she gets often at home just outside of Seattle. She likes halibut from the cold waters of the northwest and at the age of six she ate louvar, an extremely rare fish that I didn't taste until I was seventy-six. She proclaimed it "the best salmon I ever tasted." If she continues on that path, there are all sorts of fish and seafood that remain for her to discover.

Miles also is a pescatarian. So far he's been fairly adventuresome, having developed a liking for calamari *fritti* in addition to the fin fish served at home. He also has a budding taste for sushi. But on top of his list are mac and cheese and grilled cheese sandwiches.

Alise started as an "if you eat it so will I" kid. Early on, she sat on my lap and ate teriyaki chicken and broiled salmon. Then her tastes changed and now she won't eat any meat, poultry or fish. But if there's some good salami within reach, count her in. We'll have to wait and see where all this goes. She loves pasta, particularly with "Grandma Jennifer's special red sauce." She also loves virtually any kind of fruit or vegetables. She shares my preference for vegetables that are raw. She was still one year old when she stood on her tiptoes and stretched her little body to try to see the countertop where I was peeling and cleaning shrimp. At six she helped Lloyd prepare a brisket for the slow cooker. But when it was done and Lloyd asked if she wanted a taste, she said, "No, thank you. I'm not interested in that."

Carlie is too young to have clear preferences. Put it on the plate in front of her and she will devour it: cheese, apples, avocado, pasta, crackers, salmon, meat loaf, chicken, strawberries—just about anything. Her first favorite words while eating were *appoo* (apple) and *mo* (more). She knows what she wants and when she wants it, and she isn't shy about making it known or trying new food.

I don't know what lies ahead for each of them in the culinary world. I hope they will try different things and their preferences will be informed. I hope each of them will take a turn as the sous chef in my kitchen and that someday I can return the favor.

For the recipes in this chapter I have chosen two dishes that are favored by some or all of our grandchildren, at least for now. At these young ages, taste in food seems to be a moving target. But here are recipes for Grandma Jennifer's Baked Spaghetti with Garden Sauce and for Granddad Larry's poached salmon.

Grandma Jennifer's Baked Spaghetti with Garden Sauce

I do virtually all the cooking at home and have done for the last 30-plus years. There was a time, before the kids were in school full time and Jennifer got a job outside the house, when she prepared most of our dinners. This was one of her favorites then and one she reprises every now and again for our grandchildren.

> 1 pound spaghetti
> 1/2 cup olive oil
> 1 large onion, diced
> 2 garlic cloves, minced
> 1/2 cup carrots, diced
> 1 cup fresh tomatoes, peeled. seeded, and chopped
> 1/2 pound mushrooms, sliced
> 1/2 teaspoon salt
> 1/8 teaspoon black pepper
> 4 cups canned no-salt-added tomato sauce
> 1 tablespoon dried oregano
> Romano or Parmesan cheese, grated

Cook the spaghetti in boiling, salted water until it is to your taste. In the meantime, heat the oil in a large skillet. Add the onion, garlic, carrots, tomatoes, mushrooms, salt and pepper. Cook over medium heat 10 minutes. Add the tomato sauce and oregano and simmer, covered, 15 minutes. Drain the spaghetti well and turn it into a greased 9" x 13" baking dish. Pour the sauce over the spaghetti and mix lightly to be sure the spaghetti is sauced throughout. Sprinkle liberally with the fresh grated cheese. Bake in a preheated oven at 350 degrees until the cheese browns.

Serve with additional fresh cheese to grate over spaghetti, garlic bread and small green salad.

Makes six to eight servings

Grandpa Larry's Poached Salmon

> 1 cup dry white wine
> 1 cup water
> 1 small onion, sliced
> 1 celery stalk (with leaves) cut in 1-inch pieces
> 4 slices of fresh lemon
> several fresh dill sprigs
> 1 laurel bay leaf
> 4 salmon fillets, 6 ounces each

Put all the ingredients except the salmon into a wide, deep frying pan. Bring to a boil, reduce the heat and simmer, covered, about 15 minutes. Uncover the pan. Place the salmon, skin side down, in the poaching liquid. Return the liquid to a boil, reduce the heat, and simmer about five minutes if the liquid is completely covering the salmon. If the salmon is not fully submerged, simmer for about three minutes, turn the salmon over and simmer another two minutes. Remove the salmon from the pan with a slotted spatula. Put the salmon on a platter, cover it with plastic wrap and put it in the refrigerator until about 30 minutes before you intend to serve it.

Note: I prefer my poached salmon at room temperature. If you want to serve it warm, poach it for 10 minutes and serve it directly from the poaching liquid.

Garnish the salmon with chopped fresh dill when you are ready to serve.

Serve with cucumber-tomato relish*, cucumbers that have been marinated in rice vinegar, and/or steamed White Rose potatoes.

*See *recipe for Chicken Pita Pockets with Cucumber*

Serves four.

CHAPTER THIRTEEN
Judy

JUST JUDY
Judy at the Hollywood Bowl and Judy at the Sahara Hotel. Judy Garland was the most exciting performer I ever saw. Two nights and two performances have stayed with me through the years.

Quick. Don't stop to think. Name the three greatest popular singers of your lifetime—or, if you are under forty, your parents' lifetime.

How about Judy, Ella, Frank, or Barbra? No last names needed. It's a safe bet that at least one of them is on your list.

For me it's an easy call: Judy hands down in first place, Frank an easy second, and a tie for third between Ella and Barbra. Add chuck Berry and the tandem of Louis Prima and Keely Smith for pure excitement. I've seen each of them perform multiple times and those occasions are etched happily in my memory. But no one could drive even a sophisticated audience into as great a frenzy as quickly and totally as Judy Garland. Whether it was at Carnegie Hall, the Sahara Hotel, or the Hollywood Bowl, it didn't matter.

The buzz of anticipation in the Copa Room of the Sands Hotel in Las Vegas was electric when Frank Sinatra was on the bill. The room would be filled with celebrities and there was no telling which of his pals would show up on stage to mug with him. The tables were cleared, the lights would dim, horns would blare and the announcer would proclaim: "Ladies and gentlemen, the Sands Hotel proudly presents Mr. Frank Sinatra." Applause would fill the room and then fade with the first notes of the first song.

Ella Fitzgerald at the legendary Cocoanut Grove in the Ambassador Hotel in Los Angeles was a guaranteed full house. It would be a welcoming and jovial crowd that waited for her to take the stage. Applause after every song would be warm and appreciative. The tone in the room during dinner was as mellow as her voice.

Jennifer and I attended two of Barbra Streisand's "farewell" concerts. We paid $1,500 a seat for the first one, figuring "What the hell; this is her last concert; we'll amortize it over the rest of our lives." For the second farewell concert we paid $500 a ticket. We skipped farewell concerts three and four.

A Streisand audience waits on the edge of their collective seats, greets her enthusiastically, rises to their feet frequently, and then sits back down to wait for the next song. Chuck Berry would have his audience dancing in the aisles and Louis and Keely would make a room pulsate.

I can't count the number of times I flew to Las Vegas after work or for a weekend to catch a Sinatra show. It always was exciting and he never disappointed. For me, however, Judy was the gold standard. When a Judy Garland crowd came to its feet, it stayed there. I saw her perform more times than any other artist, but two of her shows stand out from all the others.

The first was on a rare rainy spring night at the Hollywood Bowl in Los Angeles. Windshield wipers were flapping at full speed as cars streamed into the parking lots. The seats in the amphitheater were soaked. Seventeen thousand anxious fans marched in with umbrellas aloft. We huddled together and laughed and joked at the improbability of what we were doing.

At show time, the orchestra chairs on stage remained empty. Five minutes. Ten minutes. Fifteen minutes past the scheduled show time. Still raining. Then a figure appeared on stage dressed all in black—black pants and a black top with a black sequined jacket. Judy Garland walked to the microphone and breathlessly asked, "Aren't you getting wet?"

The audience roared back as one voice, "Yes."

She asked, "Don't you want to go home and dry out?"

The audience roared, "No."

She laughed, and a man's voice yelled, "We love you, Judy."
"I love you too," she answered.
Another man's voice yelled, "We're staying."
The crowd roared again.
"Okay," she said. "Then I'll stay too."

She turned and walked off the stage to a wave of whistles and cheers. Applause was out of the question with umbrellas filling half the hands in the audience.

The stage crew moved the orchestra's seats under the protective cover of the bowl shell and wiped them dry. Soon the musicians were taking their places and the first notes of "Over the Rainbow" began the overture we all had heard so often. The Bowl exploded. Our reward for staying was a love fest. And fifteen minutes later, it stopped raining. We closed our umbrellas, put them under our seats, and had a night to remember.

When Judy would appear at the Cocoanut Grove, I would be there opening night and at least once more during the run. But it was in Las Vegas that I attended the other of my most memorable Judy performances. Vegas was a backyard playground for the young and single of Los Angeles in the 1960s. Airline service was frequent and inexpensive. We could hop on a plane after work, have dinner and see a show, gamble a little, and fly home in time to take a nap and shower before going to work the next morning. We did that often. We partied and played in those days and really believed it would last forever. It didn't, of course.

I was at the Sahara Hotel one night in the mid-1960s at the end of a three-day press tour of Metropolitan Water District facilities. The Copa Room hummed through dinner. Men in suits and women in gowns celebrated the night, not a baseball cap in sight. Then the tables were cleared, the lights dimmed, and the full sound of an orchestra playing "Over the Rainbow" floated across the room. The sound of an orchestra in a Vegas showroom was the kind of magic that no longer happens now that intimate dinner showrooms have given way to ten thousand-seat concert halls. The trumpets screamed, the violins purred, the drums rolled a penetrating beat. The crowd grew hushed. Then the voice announced, "Ladies and gentleman, Miss Judy Garland." The place erupted.

A single spotlight followed Judy as she strode to center stage, and the crowd rose—twelve hundred people standing and cheering, twenty-four hundred hands applauding wildly. It was a Judy crowd at its best and the next ninety minutes amounted to nothing less than a love affair between Judy Garland and that midweek crowd at the Sahara. We followed her through "A Foggy Day", "When You're Smiling" and the rest of the repertoire. And then came "Rock-a-Bye", the first of the five songs with which she traditionally closed her shows. Something special clicked that night, and when Judy's head tipped back and she raised the microphone in the air and sang the closing words "with a Dixie mel-o-deee", screams of unrestrained joy rang through the darkened room. I don't know how or when I got there, but suddenly I found myself standing on top of a table, yelling, screaming and waving a cloth napkin in the air. I looked around and found dozens of others doing the same thing. That refined crowd, dressed to the nines, had lost all control. People were on the tabletops, or standing on chairs, jumping up and down and screaming. Judy Garland is the only person I've ever seen who could do that to a crowd.

It was several minutes before Judy was able to quiet the room. Then she went right into "Over the Rainbow". I had climbed down from the tabletop and was standing along with everyone else in the room. We would not sit down again until we reached the blackjack tables after the show.

It's been more than half a century since that night in Vegas and it still brings tears to my eyes when I think of it.

On the way to the golf course recently, I was listening to a Judy Garland recording on the car stereo, an abridged version of her legendary Carnegie Hall concert. Years ago I discovered there are certain songs Judy sings better if I help her. So we were driving along—Judy and me—belting out "Rock-a-Bye". When we finished and the applause died down, we went into "Over the Rainbow". More accurately, Judy went into "Over the Rainbow". I got to the end of the first line and I was back in the Copa Room in the 1960s. Tears filled my eyes and I choked up so much that I couldn't get the words out. She was half way through the song before I could resume our duet.

Judy Garland was in a class by herself among female performers. Even her television shows left an indelible mark, whether she was in clown makeup singing "A Couple of Swells" or captivating the nation with "The Battle Hymn of The Republic" after the assassination of President John Kennedy.

When I think of Judy today or listen to one of her recordings, it's with a mixture of joy and sadness, a joy born of the number of times I was fortunate enough to see her perform and the happy memories she gave me and a sadness that comes from the realization that she left us too soon, that my sons never got the chance to see her, that my grandchildren will know her only as someone their grandfather used to like. But they will get to hear her on my original copy of the Carnegie Hall LP, and I will tell them that Great Grandma Norma, who none of them ever knew, that she could sing like that too.

Las Vegas defined cool, class and style in the late 1950s and the 1960s. If you were lucky enough to have been there you'll recognize the following. If not, sit back and turn your imagination loose.

It's four o'clock in the afternoon at the Sands, or Sahara,

or Desert Inn. You're in the casino and everyone is dressed in nice sports clothes – men in pressed trousers and sports shirts and jackets, women in skirts and blouses. No one is in jeans, or sandals. About four thirty, people start to drift away from the tables, and the swimming pool chairs begin to empty.

Then, at six o'clock, the elevators return to the main floor. Men in suits and ties, women in gowns or cocktail dresses and jewels step from the elevators and make their way to the showroom. Booze is poured. Glasses clink. Beef stroganoff or short ribs or steaks are set before diners. By eight o'clock, the dinner tables are cleared. The lights go down. The drums start to roll and the mellow sound of trumpets give out the notes of songs with which we are so familiar. In the main showrooms are the giants of the time: Frank, Judy, Dean, Sammy ... The excitement is thick enough to touch, no matter how frequently you've been there.

After the show, the crowd shifts back to the casinos and the lounges. The air crackles. Louie Prima and Keely Smith are playing the lounge at the Sahara. You are at the blackjack or craps tables and Louie and Keely are wailing. No charge. Don Rickles is holding court in the lounge at the Sands.

Unfortunately, memories are all that's left of those fabulous times. It doesn't happen like that anymore. The entertainers who could create that kind of electricity today don't play to those small rooms. Instead they focus on stadium-style concerts, and the hotels fill their showrooms with magic shows and circus acts that play to crowds in jeans and T-shirts.

On the other hand, the number of world-class restaurants in Vegas has rocketed. World-famous chefs fill the hotels on the Strip with a dazzling roster of great eateries as never before.

There are two recipes that come to my mind for this chapter as I recall those glorious times in Vegas. The first is Beef Stroganoff, the entree I ordered that night at the Sahara with Judy Garland. The second is one of my personal favorites:

the chicken livers and eggs breakfast they used to serve at the Flamingo Hotel. So here, with a tip of the cap to the good fortune that allowed me to be part of that magical time, are my recipes for those two dishes.

Beef Stroganoff Marsala

> 2 pounds boneless sirloin or round steak
> 1/2 cup butter, divided
> 4 small brown onions, thinly sliced
> 1 1/4 pounds mushrooms, sliced
> 2 tablespoons tomato paste
> 2 cups sour cream
> 1 1/2 teaspoons salt
> 1/2 teaspoon pepper
> 1/2 cup Marsala wine
> 3 cups cooked broad egg noodles

Slice the beef against the grain into strips 1/4-inch thick. Melt half the butter in a skillet until it is very hot but not brown. Add the beef and cook, tossing lightly, until the beef is browned on both sides. Remove the beef, and add half the remaining butter. When the butter is melted and very hot, add the onions and sauté for 10 minutes, stirring occasionally to prevent burning.

Remove the onions. Add and melt the remaining butter. Add the mushrooms, and sauté them for five minutes. Return the beef and onions to the skillet with the mushrooms. Add the tomato paste, sour cream, salt and pepper. Mix thoroughly. Cover and cook over low heat for 30 minutes, or until the beef is tender. Add the Marsala wine and simmer five minutes longer. Serve over a bed of noodles that have been prepared according to package directions.

Serves six.

Chicken Livers and Eggs

> Olive oil (not extra virgin)
> 1 small brown onion, thinly sliced
> 1/2 cup water, divided
> 1/4 pound mushrooms, thinly sliced
> 1/2 pound chicken livers, washed and trimmed of fat and gristle
> salt
> 4 eggs

Heat 2 tablespoons of oil in a medium frying pan. Sauté the onions until lightly browned. Add 1/4 cup of water. Cover the pan and stew the onions over medium-low heat about 15 minutes.

Add the mushrooms and stir for about one minute. Add another 1/4 cup of water. Set the temperature to low, cover, and stew the mushrooms and onions about 10 minutes.

Add the chicken livers. Stir to brown on all sides for about 5 minutes. Sprinkle the livers lightly with salt. Add a little water if the liquid is gone or almost gone. Cover and stew about 10 more minutes.

Serve with fried or poached eggs and fried potatoes or tomatoes.

Serves two.

CHAPTER FOURTEEN

La Divina

L.A. MUSIC CENTER
Jennifer and I had our first date at the Dorothy Chandler Pavilion of the Los Angeles Music Center. We celebrated our twenty-fifth and fortieth wedding anniversaries at luncheons in this building. We are season subscribers and patrons of the L.A. Opera, which performs here.

SHRINE AUDITORIUM
The only time I saw Maria Callas perform live was at the Shrine Auditorium in Los Angeles. It was on my thirty-fifth birthday during La Divina's final tour before she retired.

METROPOLITAN OPERA HOUSE
This theater was opened in 1965 and still is called "The New Met" (Metropolitan Opera House). Jennifer and I have been fortunate to attend many performances here during visits to New York.

LA SCALA
A lifelong dream came true when Jennifer and I, along with our cousins Barry and Beverly, attended a performance of La Bohème *at La Scala in Milan, Italy.*

VERONA ARENA
The night after we saw La Bohème *at La Scala we were thrilled by a performance of* Nabucco *at the arena in Verona, Italy.*

The first love of my opera life was Maria Callas, "La Divina." I listened to my mother's recordings of Callas on the phonograph in our Brooklyn apartment when I was just five or six years old. I heard her sing as a guest on radio programs in the 1940s and later saw her on *The Ed Sullivan Show* on TV. Sullivan had other opera singers on his show, but for some reason Callas was the one who grabbed me.

My all-time favorite soprano is Mirella Freni. My favorite opera recording is Freni and Luciano Pavarotti singing *La Bohème* at La Scala in 1969. I've listened to it scores of times and still, when she sings certain notes, I feel a sweet ache in the pit of my stomach.

I've had other favorites through the years. I could listen all day to Renata Tabaldi, Renata Scotto, or Aprile Millo. And now there are Anna Netrebko and Sondra Radvanovsky, who make this a wonderful time to be an opera fan.

But Callas has a special, sentimental place in my opera heart. She was my first. She was the Judy Garland of the opera stage when it came to the love showered on her by her fans.

I saw my first opera just a few weeks before my fifth birthday. My mother's father—Grandpa Max—picked me up at our Brooklyn apartment and took me to the Metropolitan Opera. Family legend has it that the opera was either *Aida* or *Rigoletto*. My grandfather died many years ago and my mother, who also is gone, never was certain which opera it was. A search of the Met archives didn't settle the matter, as both operas were performed in the same month of April, 1944, just a few weeks before my birthday.

The point is, no matter which opera it was, I became a fan. I could not have followed the story at that age, but I can recall the spectacle of it all—the costumes, the orchestra, the sets, the music, the people all dressed up in their finery, the lights of Manhattan. After that night I became more appreciative of the opera records my mother played on the Victrola and more attentive to the Saturday broadcasts from the Met.

All this laid the foundation from which I became a fan of Maria Callas, a voice and a personality for the ages. She may have been the greatest actress to ever sing on the opera stage at a time before opera directors and audiences came to expect their singers to act. Now acting is part of a singer's training. We saw Netrebko in a Los Angeles Opera performance of *Romeo et Juliette* that I'll never forget. It was clear evidence of how things have changed in the opera world.

I didn't have many opportunities to see Callas perform. We lived in Los Angeles, where opera was a novelty. She appeared here only twice, both times in concert, never in a fully staged opera. There also was the matter of her long banishment from the Met because of a feud with the management. That meant I didn't hear her on Saturday broadcasts either. But when I knew she was appearing on that week's *Ed Sullivan Show*, there was nothing that could have kept me away from the television set.

Sometime in the early 1970s, I told Jennifer there were four things I would love to be able to do again. Judy Garland already had died and Ebbets Field in Brooklyn had been torn down, so those couldn't be on the list. I wanted to see Richard Burton do Arthur's soliloquy in *Camelot* one more time. I wanted to see Yul Brynner once more as the king of Siam in *The King and I*. I wanted to see Robert Morse again in *Stop the World I Want to Get Off.* And I wanted to see Maria Callas perform.

My wish already had come true regarding Brynner and Morse when I read in the newspaper in late 1973 that Maria Callas would be doing an American concert tour the following year. No schedule was announced, but I told Jennifer, "We're going to see her wherever she performs closest to Los Angeles." I suspected that might be San Francisco.

(As for the Burton wish, we had tickets for a *Camelot* revival with Burton, but he took ill and a substitute stepped in, so we returned the tickets.)

When the schedule for the Callas tour was announced, Los Angeles was on it. Not just on the schedule, but on my birthday.

If you aren't an opera fan and want a quick lesson in what opera is all about—the emotion and drama that makes it special—try listening to a recording of Maria Callas singing "La Momma Morte" from *Andrea Chenier*. It's the aria to which Tom Hanks performed the powerful ballet scene with the intravenous stand in the movie *Philadelphia*. Make sure you have a good sound system. Lay your head back, close your eyes and rest your hands on your lap. If you have an ounce of passion in your soul, before she is finished your skin will tingle, your hair will stand on end and tears will fill your eyes.

I bought tickets for the Los Angeles Callas concert early—front row, first balcony. It would be Jennifer and me and my parents celebrating my thirty-fifth birthday.

I was in a semi-daze on the day of the performance. As I pulled into the parking lot, tears filled my eyes. I couldn't talk. I sat uncommonly silent as I waited for the performance to begin. Then, when Callas walked on the stage, I sobbed and skipped a breath. After all the years of waiting, it was finally happening; Callas was singing and I was there. It didn't matter that her voice was beyond its peak. I'm not an expert on the technical proficiency of the singing. It was Callas and nothing else mattered. My applause was for all she represented as an artist and as a personality. My cheers were for the decades of pleasure she had given me.

Maria Callas sang only eleven times in public after that night—just once more in the United States. Then she retired. I didn't know at the time it was a farewell tour. I'm not sure anyone did. It wasn't billed that way.

Opera has given me pleasure beyond measure. The dates when I was single; the times I was with my mother; the nights when Jennifer and I sat side by side at the Met, or in Milan, Verona, San Francisco, or Los Angeles.

And it all began with Callas.

Many years after Maria Callas died, I was watching a biography about her on television and learned that during a brief residency in Brooklyn she attended the same elementary school at which I later would be a student. I wonder if I might have been in the same classroom as she had been: maybe I sat at the same desk as the future diva from Greece. Here, as a tribute to Maria Callas and the special joy she and opera have given me, is a recipe for the only Greek dish I ever prepared.

Moussaka

```
salt
2 eggplants, peeled and sliced about 1/2 inch thick
1 pound ground lamb
1 medium onion, chopped
1 pint tomato sauce
1 tablespoon dried oregano
1 tablespoon dried thyme
1/2 teaspoon cinnamon
2 tablespoons extra virgin olive oil
3/4 stick butter
3/4 cup flour
1/2 quart hot milk
2 eggs, beaten
1/2 teaspoon nutmeg
```

Set the eggplant slices on a rack over a rimmed baking pan. Sprinkle salt lightly on both sides of the eggplant slices. After 30 minutes, wash off the salt and pat the slices dry with a paper towel.

Mix together the lamb, onion, tomato sauce, oregano, thyme and cinnamon in a wide frying pan. Simmer covered until most of the liquid is gone. While the meat mixture is cooking, fry the eggplant slices in the olive oil in a separate pan.

Melt the butter in a saucepan. Stir in the flour and cook over medium-low heat to brown the flour. Add the milk, beaten eggs and nutmeg, stirring with a whisk as you do. Cook the sauce slowly, continuing to stir until thickened.

Place the meat mixture in a deep baking dish. Layer the eggplant on top of the meat. Pour the sauce over the eggplant.

Bake in a preheated 500-degree oven until browned. Check it after 10 minutes to see if it's ready. If not, give it a few more minutes. Cut into thick squares to serve.

Serve with a small green salad in vinaigrette dressing and topped with feta cheese.

Serves four.

CHAPTER FIFTEEN
Fantasies

OLYMPIC GOLD
I became a fan of Olympic and World Champion figure skater Peggy Fleming the first time I saw her skate on TV. Even at that young age, she exuded style and class. In 1968 she won Olympic Gold.

PEGGY AND GREG
My admiration for Peggy Fleming has grown through the years of seeing her skate and hearing her as a commentator during TV broadcasts of skating competitions. My latest Peggy Fleming fantasy: to see an opera and have dessert with her and her husband, Greg.

A man's fantasies tend to change as he gets older.

Early in life, probably starting as a preteen, a boy in the 1950s or '60s might have fantasized about a photo in *Playboy*, or the swimsuit issue of *Sports Illustrated*, or even just an ad in the newspaper.

These days there's far less chance of there being a newspaper in the house and the boy is much more likely to have to rely on passing images of Victoria's Secret ads on TV or in catalogues delivered in the mail.

Those boyhood fantasies are largely uninformed, with some vague awareness that there is such a thing as sex. Later, in his early teens, armed with all sorts of devices with which to access the internet, he's likely to track down more explicit stuff on websites. That's when girls his own age, or maybe a little older, take their places in the expanded horizons of his fantasies, which by then probably are a tad more informed or at least more explicit.

Still later, as a young man, his fantasies may turn into scenes from plays that build on something that actually happened. There even may be a hint of romance. Take, for instance, the time I met the late, astoundingly beautiful actress, Natalie Wood. As I described in Chapter 8—Convertible Cars and Celebrity Bars—it was a brief and very casual encounter. We met when we were going to different meetings in the same *Life* magazine offices in Beverly Hills. The fantasy would come later, when I asked myself what might have happened if I had been less in awe of her and asked her to dinner. After all, there was a basis for the fantasy; she wasn't just pictures on a screen. We actually met and spoke and we each were unmarried. It was a time before bodyguards and security concerns. She might have said, "Yes," and where might that have led? That's the kind of harmless fantasy men have a thousand times in their lives.

Then there are the later-in-life fantasies, when a man forgets he's in his sixties or seventies and allows himself to believe he might still have a chance with a woman in her twenties or thirties. I laughed about this recently as I walked through Macy's department store on the way from my office to lunch at the mall across the street. I try to keep a welcoming smile on my face wherever I am. Often, as I walk through the department store some of the saleswomen will say "hello" and smile back. I could fool myself and think, *Damn, seventy-nine years old and I've still got it.* More likely, they are thinking, *What a nice old man.*

All this leads us to the longest running fantasy of my life. It involves Olympic and World figure-skating champion Peggy Fleming. From a distance I have viewed her not only as a beautiful woman, but also a woman of apparent substance and quality of character. This fantasy has changed many times over the years. The latest version goes like this: Jennifer and I are in San Francisco to attend a performance of the opera *Samson and Delilah* at the War Memorial Opera House. After dinner we take a taxi to the opera house. We take our seats — center orchestra, row H — and soon a couple is seated next to us. I glance over and there she is, Peggy Fleming, sitting right next to me. We chat for a few minutes before the opera. She introduces me to her husband and I introduce them to Jennifer. At intermission, we chat some more. She is flattered that I remember the music to which she skated when she won Olympic Gold — "Mon Coeur S'Ouvre à Ta Voix" from *Samson and Delilah*. I ask if she and her husband would like to join us for dessert after the performance. Of course, since it's a fantasy, they say, "Yes." We have a pleasant time together, become friends and the four of us continue to see each other through the years.

Now, that's a far cry from my earlier Peggy Fleming fantasies, when her husband and my wife were nowhere in sight.

The first time I saw her (do I call her Peggy Fleming every time, or can I call her Peggy for the rest of this chapter?) was in a televised skating performance in 1964, when she won the U.S. Figure Skating Championship. She was sixteen and clearly too young for my fantasies. But I saw something special in that teenage girl—a combination of elegance, style and grace that set her apart.

Two years later, the sixteen-year-old girl had grown into a lovely woman. (Beautiful would come later, with maturity.) When she skated to the aria from *Samson and Delilah*, I was enchanted. I remember thinking at the time *what a classy young woman she must be to select this music.* When she was interviewed after she completed her skating program, she spoke with poise and intelligence, none of the empty palaver we frequently hear from other skaters. I have been a fan ever since.

I was a sportswriter back then and probably could have arranged to meet Peggy. But I didn't operate that way. If we happened to meet, fine. I wasn't covering her skating performances and it wouldn't have felt right. Besides, she was only eighteen, and I was nine years older than she was. Next thing I knew, she was twenty-two and married. Actually, she married Greg just eighty-four days after Jennifer and I were married. I joked that she decided there was no sense waiting for me anymore.

Jennifer learned early in our time together how much I enjoyed figure skating and of my particular appreciation for Peggy Fleming. As we watched Peggy skate and listened to her commentary on broadcasts, Jennifer also became a fan to the point where she could recognize Peggy's voice before seeing her, just as I could.

Decades have rolled by since then. Peggy's a grandmother now and I'm a grandfather. Still, everyone who knows me knows of my Peggy Fleming fascination. I get teased about it, even by Jennifer. But that's okay. It's all harmless fun. If I'm going to be teased about something it might as well be Peggy Fleming.

The first time I saw Peggy Fleming in person was in the summer of 1997. She was participating in a memorial tribute to the late Carlo Fassi, who coached her and many other top skaters. All the receipts from that evening went to a fund for his young children. The performance was at Lake Arrowhead, a training mecca for world-class skaters in the mountains about an hour and a half east of Los Angeles. It was an emotional night for the skaters. They were there because they couldn't imagine not being there. They were skating not for money or notoriety but out of love and respect for Fassi and what he meant to each of them and to their art.

When Peggy first appeared on the ice as an on-camera commentator, the crowd and the other skaters greeted her with enthusiasm and affection. When it was her time to skate, the other skaters lined the rail and watched with reverence. She was the queen and the spotlight was hers. It was clear from her comportment, however, that she thought of herself not as a queen, but as one of a group tied together by the sport they love. During her performance, with the audience focused on her and only her, she skated by her youngest son, who was seated in the front row, and she blew him a kiss. I smiled, and tears filled my eyes. After all those years, she was still able to perform and entertain, I was there and I thought how wonderful it was that this youngster could have a chance to see that so many people thought his mother was special.

Just a few months later, during the 1998 Winter Olympics, the world was told that Peggy Fleming had breast cancer and would undergo surgery. The dignity with which she handled the announcement and her subsequent public discussions of her illness were true to the class and character I detected in that young woman all those years before. Whatever her private fears and inner thoughts, to the public she showed resolve, never the victim, never seeking sympathy.

As a mature woman now, she speaks of her younger years with humility and humor. She tells how her family "didn't have as much money as some of the other skaters" and how she knew there was nothing she could do about it, so "I just had to jump higher and spin faster." She talks of her mother sewing her costumes and her father making the ice on which she practiced. And I can hear the love and appreciation she has for what they did.

There are thousands of performers who reach the top or near the top of their art or sport. Usually it is through a single-minded devotion to practice and performing. Often the drive and dedication to succeed narrows the person. Not so with Peggy Fleming. When I first saw her as a young girl, I saw someone who seemed more complete, more grounded, if you will. When I watched her as a young woman, I thought I saw someone to whom skating was an important part of life but not life itself. Now, in her maturity and classic elegance, I see I was right.

Here's a question for you women readers. If you knew your husband had a longtime fascination with another woman, would you do something to remind him of her? Well, for one of my birthdays, Jennifer gave me a gift of Peggy Fleming's autobiography, *The Long Program: Skating Toward Life's Victories*. We had a good laugh about it and then we each read the book.

Our admiration for Peggy grew. The photo of Peggy on the cover of that book is fabulous—not something many women would want their husbands looking at. But the whole incident was in perfect harmony with the seriousness, or lack of same, with which we all treat my "Peggy Fleming thing".

Since this whole Peggy Fleming fascination is a fantasy, there obviously is no food I can directly associate with her. Since in my current fantasy we go for dessert after the opera, I decided this chapter would be devoted to dessert recipes. So, here they are, a few dessert recipes—none of which have I shared with Peggy Fleming or her husband, before or after an opera, except in the fantasy. But who knows? Maybe someday.

Cheesecake

> **Crust**
> 1 1/2 cups graham cracker crumbs (about 14 crackers, finely crumbled)
> 1/4 cup sugar
> 1/4 cup unsalted butter, softened

Combine the cracker crumbs, sugar, and butter thoroughly. Pat the mixture into a 9-inch pie pan.

> **Filling**
> 12 ounces cream cheese (not whipped)
> 2 eggs, beaten
> 1 teaspoon lemon juice
> 1 teaspoon grated lemon rind
> 3/4 cup sugar
> 2 teaspoons vanilla extract

Combine all the ingredients in a mixing bowl. Beat with a hand mixer until the mixture is light and frothy. Pour the mixture into the crust and bake at 350 degrees for 30 minutes. Remove the pie from oven and cool for 5 minutes.

> **Topping**
> 1 cup sour cream
> 3 tablespoons sugar
> 1 teaspoon vanilla extract

Mix all the ingredients together. Spread the mixture over the top of the pie. Return the pie to the oven and bake 10 more minutes. Remove the pie from the oven and let it cool for 15–20 minutes. Refrigerate for 5 hours or more before serving.

Biscuit Tortoni

I found this in my mother's handwriting in a recipe box. It's kind of showy and never fails to get rave reviews from our dinner guests.

> 3 eggs
> 1/2 cup sugar
> 1 cup heavy cream
> 1/2 cup crushed almond cookies or macaroons, divided
> 1/2 cup chopped toasted almonds
> 2 teaspoons vanilla extract
> 2 tablespoons sweet sherry or Grand Marnier (optional)

In a large mixing bowl, beat the eggs and sugar until light and lemon colored. Whip the heavy cream and fold it into the bowl along with 1/4 cup of the crushed cookies, the almonds, vanilla and the sherry or Grand Marnier, if using. Pour the mixture into 4-ounce fluted paper cups or dessert cups. Sprinkle with remaining 1/4 cup of crumbled cookies. Freeze until firm. If you are going to keep this for more than a few hours, cover the dessert with plastic wrap.

Makes about fourteen 4-ounce servings.

Latticed Apple Pie

> 2 prepared, uncooked 9-inch pie crusts
> 6 cups peeled, sliced Gala, Granny Smith, Gravenstein, or other cooking apples
> 1 cup sugar
> 1 teaspoon ground cinnamon

Mix the apples, sugar and cinnamon in a large bowl until the apples are well coated. Turn the mixture into one of the pie crusts.

Remove the other crust from its pie tin. Roll it out with a lightly flowered rolling pin and cut it into strips 1/2 inch wide. Place one strip across the top of the pie filling. Place a second strip across the first to form an X. Working from the middle out, continue to weave overlapping strips about 1/2 inch apart to form a loosely woven pattern. With moistened fingertips, press the ends of the strips to seal the lattice into the edge of the pie shell. Bake in a preheated oven at 375 degrees for 45 minutes, until apples are cooked and the crust is golden brown.

Strawberry Glaze Pie

> 2 quarts strawberries, hulled, divided
> 1 1/3 cup water, divided
> 1 cup sugar
> 3 tablespoons cornstarch
> 1 10-inch baked pie crust
> 1 cup heavy cream, whipped

Mash 1 cup of strawberries and combine with 1 cup of water in a saucepan. Boil for 5 minutes. Dissolve the cornstarch with the remaining 1/3 cup of water. Add the sugar and cornstarch to the saucepan with the mashed strawberries. Boil for about 5 minutes, stirring constantly, until the or mixture turns clear.

Remove from the heat, and allow the glaze to cool.

Add the remaining strawberries to the glaze and toss gently to coat. Arrange the strawberries in the pie shell and refrigerate.

Serve with whipped cream topping.

Note: For ease of arranging the strawberries in the pie shell, it's a good idea to slice a number of them in half before putting them into the glaze.

CHAPTER SIXTEEN
Mothers and Daughters and Others

EDIE AND THE GIRLS *Daughter-in-law Edie with granddaughters Carlie (left) and Alise (right)*

JULIE AND ELLA *Daughter-in-law Julie with granddaughter Ella, watching grandson Miles' soccer practice*

JACQUI IRWIN *California State Assemblymember*

ANDRA HOFFMAN *Trustee, Los Angeles Community College District*

They carried their trays to a table in the food court at the Fashion Square Mall in Sherman Oaks, California. It's across the street from my old office in the San Fernando Valley area of Los Angeles. I used to eat lunch there several times each week. One day I noticed two women, well-dressed in the casual way that defines Los Angeles style: designer clothing and tasteful jewelry for a few hours of lunch and shopping. It's that kind of mall.

L.A., you see, is a giant gene pool of attractive people. For more than one hundred years some of the best-looking people in the world have poured into the city, hoping to be "discovered". Most of them were not discovered, but stayed on anyway. Over the decades these attractive people met, merged, and procreated. You can see the result virtually everywhere you turn, including the Fashion Square Mall.

From their interaction I guessed the two women might be a mother and her daughter. One looked to be in her late twenties or early thirties, the other in her late forties or early fifties. Their conversation was animated, with delightful facial expressions and easy hand gestures. They were fully involved with each other as they talked and smiled and ate. I doubt they were aware of me stealing glances at them.

That was the day, about twenty years ago, that I first realized, *This business of getting older can broaden a man's perspective in some delightful ways.* It also was the day the seed was planted that grew into this book.

As a younger man, I probably would have looked right by the mother and been interested only in the daughter. Now, much later in life, I found both women compelling. Through my twenties I was attracted to women as young as eighteen or nineteen and as old as thirty or thirty-one. My focus changed as I added years to my life. Now my head can be turned by the class, style, poise and loveliness of a woman of any age. And my definition of loveliness has evolved.

No man can resist the impulse to let his eyes follow an attractive woman. But the ones who have stayed in my life, attractive though they might be, have far more going for them.

As I roar through my seventies and get ready to crash into 80, I have women friends who are as much as thirty years younger than I am. Fortunately, I also have a very understanding wife, who has grown accustomed to the fact that I like women more than I like men.

That's been true since my teenage years. From my earliest days I found most girls and women to be more open and genuine than most men. There are a number of women with whom I have lunch or dinner frequently. We talk and laugh together; we share confidences and seek advice from each other. I can think of only three men who fit that description currently and no more than five or six in my entire adult life.

At dinner several years ago, I told a woman friend, "I look at you and other women in their forties and fifties, and I see vital and attractive people. Then I realize when you look at me, you see a senior citizen."

"Oh, no," she said. "Not you."

No one ever has uttered nicer words to me.

While we're on the subject of mothers and daughters, there's an incident that occurred when I was in my late forties that forced me to admit for the first time the reality of the years that had gone by. On a flight home from a business trip to San Francisco, I came face to face with the daughter of an old girlfriend. Not some cute little girl, but a fully grown, very attractive woman.

I was seated near the front of the plane for the flight home, when my eyes were drawn to a flight attendant who was greeting passengers. *"My god,"* I thought, *"she looks just like Laurie."*

I didn't want to be intrusive, but I couldn't take my eyes off her, even after she became aware I was watching. I studied her facial expressions and her movements throughout the one-hour flight. I watched her mouth when she spoke. I watched her eyes as she poured drinks for passengers. The longer I watched, the more convinced I became that she was a high school girlfriend frozen in time.

As I was leaving the plane, I approached her. "Excuse me," I said. "I'm sorry if I made you uncomfortable. But you remind me of someone I knew in high school. Did your mother go to Burbank High?"

I could see her relax. It couldn't have been pleasant to have some strange guy sneaking looks at her for over an hour, although I expect it wasn't the first time it happened to her. I also saw the surprise on her face. Her mother had, in fact, gone to Burbank High School.

"Was her name Laurie Mattson?" I asked.

"Yes," she answered. There was a question in her eyes.

"I thought so," I said. "You look so much like her it's scary. Please tell her Larry Levine said hello."

We chatted for a few minutes. As I walked away, I thought: *I dated her mother years ago; were I not married I could have asked the daughter to dinner.* I don't know whether she would have accepted, but that's not the point. How was a guy supposed to stay young when the images from his youth were replaced by their adult daughters?

Then there was the time Jennifer and I were having dinner at a restaurant in Hollywood. I was distracted by a woman sitting in a booth opposite us.

"See that woman, the blonde in the booth by the wall?" I asked Jennifer. "She looks like an old girlfriend of mine." Then I joked, "Actually, I guess she looks like the daughter of an old girlfriend. I'm sure the old girlfriend doesn't look like that anymore."

The women you've read about so far in this book all played important roles in my personal life. But there are a number of others who straddle the line between my personal and professional lives and who have contributed to my journey in meaningful ways.

The early success of my career as a political consultant was driven by five election campaigns that elected strong women to public office.

The first was Diane Watson, a school psychologist in Los Angeles, who I met early in 1975. Diane ran for the Los Angeles Board of Education in 1973 and lost. She contacted me when she decided to give it another try two years later. Diane speaks seven languages fluently. She holds a Bachelor's Degree from UCLA and a Master's from California State University, Los Angeles. Later she earned a Doctorate in educational administration from Claremont Graduate University and attended the Kennedy School of Government at Harvard University.

Diane's campaign was the first one I ran completely on my own, without the guidance of my friend and mentor, the late Robert P. Jeans. In a different context, it has been said "you never forget your first time." Well, it's true in the context of election campaigns also. I've run more than two hundred campaigns since Diane's but hers will forever be the first.

We won that election. While protests raged across the nation against the use of school busing for integration in the spring of 1975, Diane became the first African-American woman ever elected to the Los Angeles Unified School District Board of Education. She defeated an anti-busing candidate from the most conservative area of the district.

Next was Florence Bernstein. Flo passed the bar and became an attorney later in life. In 1976, at the age of fifty-five, she decided to run for judge of the Los Angeles Municipal Court. We were introduced by a mutual friend, another political consultant, who had helped her through the Primary Election but was not able to handle the runoff later in the year.

In November, 1976 Flo became the only woman in L.A. County history to defeat an incumbent Municipal Court judge. We stayed in contact until her death in 1991, even though she never had another contested election.

I had known Wallace Albertson for seven years before she decided to run for a seat on the Los Angeles Community College District Board of Trustees in 1977. Wally was the first woman president of the California Democratic Council and the wife of actor Jack Albertson. She held a Bachelor's Degree in English from the University of Pittsburgh and a Master's in journalism from Columbia University. She had been a writer for NBC radio and TV and owned her own import/export business. When Wally asked me to handle her campaign, I was delighted.

We won the election and Wally became the first person to defeat an incumbent member of the Community College Board of Trustees. She went on to serve twelve years on the board.

Among her other achievements, Wally was co-founder of Women's Strike for Peace in 1960, she earned a Master's

Degree in speech and a Doctorate in speech communications at UCLA, served on the board of AIDS Health Care Foundation, and was a member of the California State University Board of Trustees. Wally and I remained friends and political allies until her death early in 2015.

Then came 1978 and, in the parlance of the racetrack, a daily double.

I convinced Diane Watson to run for a vacant seat in the California State Senate rather than seek re-election to the school board the following year. We won the Primary Election in June and later that year she was elected as the first African-American woman ever to serve in the California state senate.

As for the second leg of that daily double, I was getting ready to leave our apartment to attend a campaign fundraising event for Diane one Sunday in January of 1978 when the telephone rang and the voice on the other end said, "I'm-Sally-Tanner-I'm-running-for-Assembly-in-the-Sixtieth-district-I'm-going-to-win-and-everyone-says-I-should-talk-to-you."

She said it as if it were one long word, so fast that all I could answer was, "I beg your pardon."

She repeated the one-long-word, only a little more slowly. We arranged to meet later that day. To this day, we remain friends.

After winning the Primary Election by nearly twenty-five hundred votes against six other candidates, Sally went on in the General Election to become the first woman ever elected to represent the San Gabriel Valley in the state legislature. In 1982 Assembly Speaker Willie Brown created a new Committee on Environmental Safety and Toxic Materials in the Assembly and appointed Sally as the first chair of that committee. She held that post until she retired in 1992 after serving fourteen years in the legislature.

The role of women in my professional success didn't end in 1978. More recently, two other remarkable women won public office and are carving out their own reputations for outstanding public service.

Jacqui Irwin was a member of the City of Thousand Oaks Planning Commission when I met her in 2004 and agreed to direct her campaign for city council. She had been an Academic All-American swimmer in college and earned her degree in systems engineering. She worked on the Trident missile program. We won that first election and Jacqui became the only Democrat to serve on the Thousand Oaks city council in twenty-five years. I helped her through two subsequent re-election campaigns. Then I guided her to a 2014 Primary Election campaign victory that sent her on to become the first Democrat ever to represent her district in the State Assembly. Our bond of friendship means far more to me than our professional relationship.

Next came Andra Hoffman. We met in April 2013, and I liked her instantly. Her personal story was compelling. Eighteen years earlier she was a divorced mother of two young children, with no job, no degree, and a mountain of debt. She returned to college, while working full time and raising two children. She earned Bachelor's and Master's Degrees and became a professor of political science at a local community college. She also ran the welfare-to-work program at her campus and directed the student job placement office.

In March 2015, on a budget of just $55,000, she was elected

to the Los Angeles Community College Board of Trustees. We defeated an opponent who was part of a slate of candidates backed by an $800,000 campaign and I added a new friend to my life.

Quite a group, huh? Talk about high achievers. But there are more.

Amanda Susskind is one of my most trusted friends. I was the consultant for her campaign for state assembly in 2000, which we lost by a razor-thin margin. She moved on to practice public law and then became the Southwest Regional Director of the Anti-Defamation League. Amanda is quick with a pun and highly motivated toward public service. We've shared uncountable dinners together, usually at one of our favorite sushi bars. She gave me one of the proudest moments of my life when Jennifer and I suggested we take her to any restaurant of her choice to celebrate her fiftieth birthday and she asked, instead, if I would cook for her at our home.

Lisa Hansen is my go-to person when I need advice about something in a political campaign, I want to bounce an idea off someone, or I just feel like talking to someone very nice and very smart. Lisa walked into my office for a job interview in November 1999. She and her husband, Jim Dunn, had just moved to Los Angeles so Jim could pursue a career as a TV writer. Lisa had been involved in election campaign work in Minnesota. She seemed bright and personable. We hired her to be the day-to-day manager of Amanda's Assembly campaign, a highly visible race in one of the most highly visible districts in the state. It would have been a daunting challenge for anyone. It was doubly so for someone new to the area.

Over the course of the campaign I developed a respect for Lisa's intelligence and dry sense of humor. In a room full of people she is likely to see the bottom line in a discussion before anyone else. At the time of this writing, she is chief of staff to Los Angeles City Councilmember Bob Blumenfield. At countless dinners and lunches through the years, we have developed a friendship that I value greatly. After all these years, the quickness of her mind and her wit still catch me off guard on occasion.

Nancy Dolan is simply the best fundraiser and campaign finance director I've ever known. The thought of consulting on a campaign in which she is not involved all but freezes me. Nancy left a career as a criminal defense attorney to get involved in politics in Massachusetts. I met her in 2001, after she had moved to Los Angeles and was guiding the fundraising operation for one of my clients. We have been friends, confidants and dinner companions ever since. Nancy is smart, laughs easily and knows just about everything you'd want to know about New England seafood and shore dinners.

Tracey Poirier has been the key member of my staff and a close friend for nearly two decades. We met while she was volunteering in the headquarters of a campaign I was directing.

When my mother died, it was Tracey who stepped up and arranged the reception for friends and relatives at our house after the funeral service. When I had my emergency coronary bypass surgery in the middle of the 2008 election season, it was Tracey who kept things under control in the office while I mended at home. No client ever had reason to question the stability of our operation. In the rough and tumble of many political campaigns and the joys and stresses of two personal lives, Tracey and I have forged a deep bond of trust and friendship.

There's an old saying: A daughter is a daughter for life, but a son is a son until he finds a wife. It isn't very flattering but too often it is true. Not so for Jennifer and me. Each of our sons married strong, intelligent women. Yet I could not ask for a closer, more respectful adult relationship with either Lloyd or John.

My move into father-in-law-hood had its rough beginnings, which were not made less real by the fact that I joked about it.

John, the younger of our two sons, met professional dancer Julie Birrell when they worked on the Crystal Symphony cruise ship, John as the information technology officer and Julie with the dance company. Their first date was dinner on Bali.

All through the dating lives of our two sons, Jennifer and I refrained from expressing any opinion either way about the women they brought around. When John introduced us to Julie, we liked her, but said nothing. He needed to be free to make his own decisions about where the relationship might go. Privately, we talked about how we liked the way they related to each other and the humor with which she would deflect some of John's more interesting diversions. So, when they told us they were going to be married, we were happy.

The wedding was a wonderful affair at a hotel in Los Angeles. Julie's family and some friends flew in from her native England. Many of John's and Julie's friends from the ship came to town.

It took me nearly a year to be able to say "daughter-in-law." It wasn't that I didn't like Julie or was anything less than happy for the two of them. My tongue just wouldn't do it. John was my youngest son. If he was old enough to get married, what did that say about me? When speaking of Julie, the best I could manage was, "My son's wife." That made it more about them and not about me.

Eventually I got over it. Then, a few years later, John and Julie became parents, and the word *"granddaughter"* entered my life. I couldn't say that one either. Grandfathers were old guys. That wasn't me. So I spoke of Ella as "my son's daughter." I got over that one before she learned to say "Granddad."

Lloyd, the older of our two sons, met Edie Lambert on a flight from Seattle to Sacramento. Lloyd had been in Issaquah, just outside of Seattle, for Thanksgiving at John and Julie's home. Edie spent Thanksgiving with her family in Seattle. Lloyd was a member of the California State Assembly at the time and Edie was an anchor at the number-one TV news station in the Sacramento market. But they didn't recognize each other on the plane. By the end of the flight, they had introduced themselves and the first steps were taken toward the next family wedding.

I don't remember the first time we met Edie. I do remember that I liked her and realized she was more than just a news reader with a pretty face. But Jennifer and I stuck to our policy—no comment.

We accepted Julie and Edie into our family and our lives because they were brought to us by the sons we treasure. Now, I don't just like Julie and Edie; I love and treasure each of them also.

I marvel sometimes at the incredible good fortune that brought each of the women of *Cooking for a Beautiful Woman* into my life—not just those in this chapter but all of them in this book and others too numerous to name. The individual and collective intelligence and accomplishments of these women is astounding. That somehow each of their paths intersected with mine is in itself a thing of beauty.

As is the case with most of the recipes in the book, the recipes in this chapter are some of my personal creations from across the decades. Each calls up a memory of a special time with a special woman who allowed me to share her company. It may have been on the streets of Brooklyn, or the playgrounds of Los Angeles. It might have been on the Sunset Strip or the Vegas Strip. Maybe we were eating chicken wing gumbo at a soul food joint, or we might have been enjoying escargot or frogs legs or baked Alaska at one of the world's great restaurants. We could have been dancing a kitchen ballet in her kitchen or mine as we prepared a quiet dinner for just the two of us, or we might have been preparing to host a dinner party for friends. No matter where or when, always there was the food and the music and the laughter and the warmth. And the memories.

But no matter from where or when or with whom these recipes evolved, they all took root in that kitchen in Brooklyn those many decades ago and Mom's hand and her songs are as much a part of them as the recipes are a part of me.

Cioppino

I consider this my showcase dish. It's a long, slow recipe but the results are worth the effort. If I want to show off my cooking, this is where I turn. The monkfish can be difficult to locate, but it's what turns this into a special dish.

- 1 leek, white part only
- 2 tablespoons olive oil
- 5 cups fat-skimmed chicken broth, divided
- 4 garlic cloves, finely chopped
- 1 (14-ounce) can crushed, peeled tomatoes
- 1 cup dry red wine
- 1 teaspoon each dried and crushed thyme, basil, oregano and parsley
- 1 ounce white anchovies in olive oil
- 1/2 teaspoon salt
- 1/2 teaspoon freshly ground black pepper
- 2 large carrots, peeled and sliced into 1/4 inch rings
- 8 small mushrooms, sliced
- 8 littleneck clams
- 8 mussels
- 8 medium shell-on shrimp
- 1/2 pound monkfish, cut into bite-size pieces
- 4 large scallops cut in half horizontally
- hot pepper sauce to taste

Cut the leek into 1-inch pieces. Wash and drain. Heat the olive oil in a wide skillet. Sauté the leek in the oil until soft but not browned. Add 2 1/2 cups of chicken broth and the garlic, tomatoes, red wine, thyme, basil, oregano, parsley, anchovies, salt and pepper. Simmer slowly for one hour.

Shell the shrimp and put the shells in a saucepan with 2 cups of chicken broth. Simmer for 20 minutes. Strain the broth into a bowl or measuring cup and squeeze the liquid out of the shells. Discard the shrimp shells. Put the broth into a saucepan. Add the carrots and boil for 10 minutes. Mash the carrots coarsely and add them to the main broth along with the shrimp broth. Bring to a slow boil. Add the sliced mushrooms and simmer for 15 minutes.

Steam the clams and mussels in 1/2 cup of chicken broth. Add the monkfish to the main broth and cook at a slow boil for 5 minutes. Add the shrimp and scallops at a slow boil till the shrimp turns pink and scallops are done, about 5 minutes. Add the hot pepper sauce to taste. Add the clams and mussels in their shells and cook until they are heated, no more than one minute.

Serve with crusty French bread.

Makes four large servings.

Ceviche

> 1 pound of Rockfish*
> juice of 6 limes
> 1/4 cup olive oil
> 1 teaspoon chili oil (optional)
> 2 medium tomatoes, seeded and chopped
> 1/2 onion, diced
> 2 garlic cloves, minced
> 1/2 teaspoon chili powder (or to taste)
> 1/2 teaspoon red pepper flakes (or to taste)
> 1/4 teaspoon dried oregano
> Tabasco sauce (optional, to taste)
> 1/8 cup white vinegar

Cut the fish into bite-size pieces. Marinate in lime juice to cover for 3 hours. Do not refrigerate. Toss the fish occasionally in the lime juice to assure even cooking.

While the fish is marinating, combine all other ingredients in a glass bowl and let stand to blend flavors. Stir occasionally.

Drain the fish and rinse it in cold water. Add the fish to the other ingredients. Toss, cover, and refrigerate. Remove the ceviche from the refrigerator about 1/2 hour before you are ready to serve.

Serves nicely with tortilla chips.

Rockfish has been sold for many years as red snapper, particularly on the west coast of the United States. To my taste, west coast snapper isn't very good, but the Rockfish is excellent. You may substitute red snapper if it is from the northwest, Hawaii, or Japan.

Chicken Gumbo Soup

> 3 quarts chicken stock (preferably homemade and fat-skimmed)
> 2 tablespoons butter or olive oil
> 1 onion, diced
> 1 garlic clove, diced
> 1 cup canned peeled tomatoes
> 1 cup long-grain white rice
> 2 pounds skinless, boneless chicken thighs cut into bite-size pieces
> 10 ounces fresh okra, sliced into 1/4-inch rings
> 1/8 teaspoon cayenne
> 2 tablespoons chopped fresh parsley
> 1 1/2 teaspoons filé gumbo powder

Place the stock in a large soup pot and bring it to a boil. Heat the butter or oil in a frying pan. Add the onion and garlic and sauté until the onion is tender but not browned. Add the onion, garlic and tomatoes to the broth. Bring the pot to a boil. Add the rice. Boil slowly for 20 minutes. Add the chicken, okra and cayenne. Cook 15 minutes at a medium boil. If the okra is not tender, cook another five minutes. Add the parsley. Sprinkle 1/4 teaspoon of filé gumbo on each bowl just before serving.

Serves six.

Chicken Pita Pockets with Cucumber-Tomato Relish

> 4 tablespoons olive oil, divided
> juice of 1/2 lemon
> 1/2 teaspoon dried basil
> 1/2 teaspoon fresh parsley, chopped
> 1 teaspoon cinnamon
> 1/2 teaspoon fresh dill
> 1/4 teaspoon granulated garlic
> 1/2 teaspoon cumin
> 1 tablespoon mild curry powder
> 3 boneless, skinless chicken thighs
> 1 medium brown onion, halved and sliced
> 1/2 cup water
> 2 medium mushrooms, sliced
> 2 pita pockets, halved

Prepare a marinade by mixing together 2 tablespoons of olive oil and the next eight ingredients. Cut the chicken into half-inch cubes. Pour the marinade over the chicken in a glass bowl. Stir thoroughly to coat the chicken. Cover and marinate several hours in the refrigerator, stirring occasionally.

Bring 2 tablespoons of olive oil to high heat in a wide frying pan. Add the onion and stir until it begins to brown. Add the water and stir to scrape browned bits from the bottom of the pan. Reduce the heat to low, cover and stew for one hour. Check occasionally to be sure the water stays at a slow simmer and to stir the onions. Add more water, 1/4 cup at a time, if the water evaporates.

When the onions are deep brown and sweet smelling, tip the cover of the pan to allow the water to evaporate, about 15 minutes. Add the mushrooms and stir to mix with the onions. Replace the cover on the pan and allow the mixture to stew for 15 minutes.

Remove the cover. Return the heat to medium high. Add the chicken and stir constantly until the chicken is cooked through. In the meantime, cut two pita pockets in half and warm in the oven at 250 degrees.

Remove the chicken mixture to a serving bowl with a slotted spoon to eliminate the liquid. Serve each person 2 pita halves.

Serve with cucumber-tomato relish.

Serves two.

Cucumber-Tomato Relish

> 1/2 cucumber, peeled, seeded and diced
> 1 medium tomato, diced
> 2 tablespoons white vinegar
> 1 tablespoon dried dill or 2 tablespoons chopped fresh dill

Mix together all ingredients. Allow to set at least two hours to blend flavors. Longer is better. Stir occasionally.

Chicken Cacciatore

> 1/4 cup olive oil (not extra virgin)
> 2 pounds chicken thighs, bone in and skin on
> 1 cup sliced onions
> 1/2 cup chopped red bell pepper
> 1 garlic clove, minced
> 1 (28-ounce) can fire-roasted tomatoes
> 2 tablespoons fresh parsley, chopped
> 1/2 teaspoon oregano
> 1/4 teaspoon thyme
> 1/2 teaspoon salt
> dash pepper
> 1/4 pound mushrooms, sliced
> 1/4 cup dry red wine

Heat the oil in a large skillet. Add the chicken and brown on all sides. Remove the chicken and set it aside. Add the onion, red pepper and garlic to the skillet and sauté until the onion is tender but not brown.

Force the tomatoes through a food mill and add them to the skillet along with the mushrooms, parsley, oregano, thyme, salt and pepper. Cook, covered, over low heat for 15 minutes, stirring occasionally.

Add the chicken, baste with the sauce, cover and simmer. Turn the chicken after 20 minutes and simmer 10 minutes longer.

Add the mushrooms and wine. Stir them into the sauce. Cook, uncovered, about 15 minutes, until sauce is desired consistency.

Serve over white rice or with penne pasta. Be sure to spoon some sauce over the rice or pasta.

Serves two.

Chicken Fricassee

Geography question: *What's the difference between chicken cacciatore and chicken fricassee?*
Answer: *The Alps—cacciatore is Italian; fricassee is French.*

> 4 tablespoons olive oil, divided
> 6 garlic cloves, chopped
> 4 chicken legs and thighs (or 8 thighs)
> 1/4 cup all-purpose flour
> 1 pound fresh mushrooms, caps and stems separated, caps halved or quartered, stems halved lengthwise
> 1 can (28 ounces) fire roasted Roma tomatoes, well drained and halved
> salt and freshly ground black pepper to taste
> 1/4 cup fresh parsley, chopped

Heat 3 tablespoons of oil in a large frying pan over medium heat. Add the garlic. Reduce the heat to low and sauté the garlic, stirring frequently, until softened but not browned, about 2 minutes. Your aim is to infuse the garlic flavor into the oil, not to cook the garlic. Remove the garlic to a small plate.

Dredge the chicken pieces lightly in flour. Raise the heat to medium high. Add the chicken pieces and brown well on all sides, about 20 minutes.

Meanwhile, heat the remaining oil in a different frying pan over medium high heat. Add the mushrooms and sauté, stirring occasionally, until lightly browned, about 5 to 6 minutes.

When the chicken is browned, stir in tomatoes, mushrooms and garlic. Season with salt and pepper. Reduce the heat to medium-low, cover and cook the chicken 20 minutes, turning it at the 10-minute mark. Uncover and cook another 10 minutes. Sprinkle with parsley.

Serve with steamed White Rose potatoes or penne pasta. Be sure to spoon some of the sauce over the potatoes or pasta.

Serves four.

Chicken Pot Pie

> 4 chicken thighs, boneless and skinless
> 1 1/2 cups chicken broth
> 2 tablespoons butter
> 1/2 cup finely diced carrots
> 1/4 cup finely diced celery
> 1/4 cup finely diced onion
> 2 tablespoons all-purpose flour
> 1/4 teaspoon dried thyme
> salt and pepper to taste
> 1/2 cup peas, frozen or fresh
> crust (see following)

Place the chicken in a saucepan with the broth. Cover and simmer for about 30 minutes. Allow the chicken and broth to cool. Cut the chicken into bite-size pieces and set it aside. Strain off one cup of broth and set it aside. (The remainder of broth can be frozen for other use.)

Melt the butter in a saucepan. Add the carrots and sauté over low heat about 5 minutes. Add the celery and onion and sauté an additional 5 minutes. Stir in the flour and cook until the flour is toasted to golden, stirring frequently to prevent burning.

Slowly add the reserved chicken broth, stirring constantly to incorporate with the floured vegetables and form a thickened sauce. Be sure to scrape the brown bits from the bottom of the pan. Add the thyme, salt and pepper and stir well. Stir in the peas and chicken. Remove the pan from the heat. Transfer the mixture to a 1 1/2-quart casserole or individual ramekins and set it aside. Drop the crust onto the chicken mixture. Bake, uncovered, at 350 degrees for 30 minutes.

> **Crust**
> 1/2 cup all-purpose flour
> 1/4 teaspoon salt
> 1/4 teaspoon sugar
> 1 teaspoon baking powder
> 2 tablespoons unsalted butter
> 5 tablespoons milk

In a mixing bowl, blend together the flour, salt, sugar and baking powder. Cut the butter into the flour mixture with two knives or a pastry blender until the mixture forms lumps like small peas. Add the milk and toss briefly with a fork until a dough is formed. Drop pieces of the dough onto the chicken. No need to smooth this into a pie crust. It will be more like a biscuit dough.

Makes two servings.

Herb-Baked Chicken

> 1/2 cup chicken broth
> 1/2 cup red wine vinegar
> 1 tablespoon fresh parsley
> 1 tablespoon dried chives
> 2 tablespoons vegetable oil
> 1 teaspoon salt
> 1/2 teaspoon dried thyme
> 1/2 teaspoon dried marjoram
> 1/4 teaspoon freshly ground black pepper
> 1/2 teaspoon cumin
> 12 fryer chicken legs and/or thighs

Place all the ingredients except the chicken in a blender. Blend for about 30 seconds. Arrange the chicken in a single layer in a baking pan. Pour the blended mixture over the chicken. Place the pan, uncovered, in a 475-degree preheated oven. Reduce the temperature to 350 degrees. Bake about one hour, turning and basting frequently. If you see the liquid is evaporating too quickly, add more chicken broth as needed.

Serve with parsleyed potatoes.

Serves six to eight.

Lemon Chicken

> 4 chicken legs and thighs (or 8 thighs)
> 1 teaspoon salt
> 1 teaspoon granulated onion
> 1 teaspoon dried thyme
> 1 teaspoon dried marjoram
> 1 tablespoon grated lemon peel
> 2/3 cup lemon juice
> 1 cup water

Rub the chicken with salt and arrange skin side down in a shallow baking dish. Combine the remaining ingredients and pour them over the chicken. Bake, uncovered, at 400 degrees for 20 minutes. Turn the chicken and bake 20 minutes longer. Baste occasionally with the pan juices.

Serve over steamed white rice with pan juices as sauce.

Serves four.

Oven Chicken and Wedge Fries

> 4 chicken legs and thighs
> salt and black pepper
> 1/4 cup butter
> 2 garlic cloves, minced
> 1/2 to 1 teaspoon chili powder (to taste)
> 1/4 teaspoon ground cumin
> 1/2 teaspoon paprika
> 1 tablespoon lemon juice
> 2 medium baking potatoes, scrubbed and each cut into eight wedges lengthwise*
> lemon slices

Season the chicken with salt and pepper to taste. Place the chicken in a large baking dish. Bake at 350 degrees for 30 minutes.

Melt the butter in a small saucepan. Stir in the garlic, chili powder, cumin and paprika. Heat for 2 minutes. Add the lemon juice. Set aside in a warm spot but not on the heat.

Place the potato wedges around the chicken pieces. Brush the chicken pieces and potato wedges with the melted butter. Return the pan to the oven and continue baking 30 to 40 minutes, until chicken and potatoes are tender, brushing both occasionally with more butter and drippings.

Place the chicken and potatoes on a serving platter and garnish with lemon slices.

Caution: Do not cut the potato wedges too thick or they will not be cooked through when the chicken is done.

Makes four servings.

Chicken Tandoori

Unless you have an actual tandoori oven in your house, which I don't, you may want to try this version as a substitute. I don't think I've ever known anyone who had a tandoori oven in his/her house.

> 8 chicken thighs and/or legs
> 1/2 cup plain yogurt
> 4 tablespoons fresh lime juice
> 1 small onion, diced
> 1 garlic clove, minced
> 1 teaspoon powdered or granulated ginger
> 1 teaspoon red pepper flakes
> 1/2 teaspoon each cinnamon, cumin and turmeric
> 1/4 teaspoon coriander

Score the chicken lightly with a sharp knife. Mix all the other ingredients together. Put everything in a plastic bag and toss to coat the chicken. Put the bag in a non-aluminum bowl. Marinate the chicken for 24 to 48 hours.

Remove the chicken from the marinade. Broil or barbeque the chicken 6 to 8 inches from the heat for 35 to 45 minutes, turning occasionally. (Alternately, bake the chicken at 350 degrees for 40 minutes. Then put it under the broiler for about 5 minutes on each side to brown.)

Serve with a vegetable-rice dish.

Serves four.

Roast Turkey with Dripping Gravy

> 1 fresh never-been-frozen turkey, free range if possible

Allow about 1 pound per person for a large party. I like to buy the biggest turkey that will fit in my oven—24 to 26 pounds—so there will be plenty of leftovers. Also, don't buy a turkey that has been butter-basted or doctored in any other way. If the bird you buy comes with an inserted thermometer, pull it out and throw it away.

The quality of the turkey on your table depends more upon the quality of the turkey you buy than on any other factor. So, compromise at your own risk.

Before we go any further, let me tell you that I like to taste the turkey free of any enhancements, adornments, or other interfering flavors. I want my turkey with turkey-dripping gravy. The rest of the flavors can come from the side dishes.

Preheat the oven to 325 degrees.

If the bird has a metal binder or anything else to hold the legs in place, remove it. Remove the heart, liver, gizzard and neck from the inside of the bird. (Save them for other uses. I'll get to that later.) Wash the bird inside and out with cold tap water. Cut away all large chunks of fat, including the butt, which my mother liked to roast to a crisp and eat. Cut away excess flaps of skin. Pat the bird dry with a paper towel. Place the bird on a rack in a roasting pan, breast side down.

Tent the bird with tinfoil, being careful that the foil doesn't touch the bird. Put the tented bird in the oven for the length of time shown on the chart below. One hour before the turkey is done, remove it from the oven. Place the turkey on a large platter. Pour the drippings from pan into a wide saucepan. Return the turkey to the rack, this time breast side up. Replace the tent over the bird and return it to the oven.

When the bird is done, remove it from the oven, remove the tent and allow the bird to set for 15 minutes before carving.

I never stuff a turkey for three reasons. First, it's easier not to have to unstuff the bird when you take it out of the oven. Second, I use the carcass for making stock and I don't want the residue of the stuffing sticking to the inside of the carcass. And third, I've heard so many stories of people getting ill from stuffing cooked inside the turkey that it scares me. However, if you insist on stuffing the bird, remove the stuffing as soon as you take the bird from the oven and put the stuffing in a warmed casserole and return it to the oven until ready to serve.

TURKEY ROASTING TIME CHART (AT 325 DEGREES)

Weight	**Stuffed**	**Unstuffed**
12–16 pounds	3 1/2–5 hrs.	3–4 hrs.
16–20 pounds	5–6 hrs.	4 1/2–5 1/2 hrs.
20–24 pounds	5 1/2–7 hrs.	5–6 1/2 hrs.
24–28 pounds	6 1/2–7 1/2 hrs.	6–7 hrs.

Dripping Gravy

> 3 cups turkey stock
> turkey pan drippings
> salt and pepper to taste (optional)
> 1/2 cup butter, or fat from the turkey drippings
> 1/2 cup all-purpose flour

Remember the turkey pan drippings we poured off? There are two ways you can skim the fat from it. The best way I found is to use the fat skimmers sold in many kitchenware shops. A 2-cup size will be enough for a smaller turkey. After pouring the drippings into the skimmer, put the skimmer in the freezer until you are ready to use the drippings. Otherwise, you can pour the drippings into a wide saucepan and put the pan in the freezer. After 15 minutes or so, drop in a few ice cubes to help congeal the fat.

About 1 hour before you plan to start carving the turkey, place the turkey stock on the stove over a medium-low heat. Don't let it boil. When the stock is heated, turn the temperature down to low.

Make a roux using the butter or the fat drippings, and flour. Stir some of the warmed stock into the roux. Then slowly pour the roux into the stockpot, stirring constantly to incorporate fully. Bring the stock to a very slow boil and stir it occasionally until it thickens. Stir in the fat-skimmed turkey drippings and heat the gravy through. Don't boil it too long or too vigorously or the gravy will break down.

Now, for the heart, liver, giblets and neck we took out of the turkey. While the turkey is roasting, put them in a saucepan with enough water to cover. Bring it to a boil, reduce the heat and let it boil slowly for about 30 minutes. Remove the heart and liver and let the giblets and neck boil for another half hour. When they are done, cut the heart, liver and giblets into small pieces, allow them to cool, and strip the meat from the neck. Give the heart, liver, giblets and neck meat to the cat. You will have a friend for life. If you don't have a cat or know someone who does, use the parts to make a stock. The water in which you boiled these parts can be added to the stock for the gravy.

Leftover Turkey Gumbo

> 2 tablespoons olive oil
> 2 small onions, diced
> 4 cups homemade turkey broth
> 2 cups canned stewed tomatoes
> 4 cups fresh okra, sliced
> 2 tablespoons chopped fresh parsley
> 1/2 teaspoon paprika
> 2 cups cooked diced turkey leftovers
> 2 teaspoons dried oregano
> 1/4 teaspoon black pepper
> Tabasco sauce to taste
> 2/3 cup long-grain white rice

Heat the oil in an 8-quart saucepan. Sauté the onions until tender but not brown. Add the broth, tomatoes, okra, parsley and paprika. Heat and simmer for 10 minutes. Add the turkey, oregano, pepper, Tabasco (to taste) and rice. Bring the pot to a slow boil for 20 minutes.

A gumbo purist will skip the rice and make a roux to thicken the dish.

Makes four to six servings.

Leftover Turkey Soup

> 8 cups turkey stock (homemade from carcass, wing tips, thigh bones, etc.)
> 1 large onion, chopped
> 2 celery stalks with leaves, chopped
> 1 carrot, diced
> 2 tablespoons chopped fresh parsley
> 1 teaspoon salt
> 1/8 teaspoon pepper
> 2 cups dried egg noodles
> 2 cups leftover turkey

Bring the stock to a boil in a 6-quart saucepan. Add the onion, celery and carrot and cook at a slow boil for 30 minutes. Add the noodles and boil slowly for 20 minutes. Add the turkey and boil for a few minutes to heat. Add the parsley just before serving.

Makes about six servings.

Beef Burgundy

> 1 1/2 tablespoons soy sauce
> 1 tablespoon all-purpose flour
> 3/4 pound beef stew meat, cut in 1 1/2-inch cubes
> 3 carrots, peeled and cut into 1-inch pieces
> 1 medium onion, sliced
> 1/2 cup thinly sliced celery
> 1 garlic clove, minced
> 1/4 teaspoon pepper
> 1/8 teaspoon dried marjoram
> 1/8 teaspoon dried thyme
> 1/2 cup dry red wine
> 1/2 cup sliced mushrooms
> 1 cup beef stock (homemade)

Blend the soy sauce and flour in a 3-quart baking dish. Toss the meat in the mixture to coat. Add the carrots, onion, celery, garlic, pepper, marjoram, thyme and red wine to the meat. Toss gently to mix. Cover tightly and simmer in a 325-degree oven for 1 hour. Add the mushrooms and stir gently again. Add the beef stock. Cover tightly and bake 1 1/2 to 2 hours longer, or until the meat and vegetables are tender.

Serve with fluffy hot rice, boiled broad egg noodles, or mashed potatoes.

Makes two generous portions.

Beef Stew

> 1 1/2 pound stewing beef
> 1/2 cup all-purpose flour mixed with salt and pepper to taste
> vegetable oil
> 1 medium sweet potato
> 5 cups beef stock, divided
> 1 yellow chili pepper, halved lengthwise, seeds and spine removed
> 1/2 teaspoon black pepper
> 1/4 teaspoon salt
> 1 teaspoon each dried marjoram and thyme
> 2 medium onions, sliced
> 2 large carrots, chunked
> 1 large russet potato, peeled, cut in bite-size chunks
> 1 turnip, peeled, cut in medium-size chunks
> 1 cup frozen green peas

Toss the meat to coat in a mixture of flour, salt and pepper. Shake off any excess flour. Heat the oil in a frying pan and brown the meat on all sides in batches so as not to overcrowd the pan.

Peel the sweet potato, cut it in half lengthwise and then cut it into two-inch pieces. Put the beef and the sweet potato in a stew pot or Dutch oven. Add approximately 2 1/2 to 3 cups of beef stock, enough to cover the meat. Add the chili pepper, black pepper and salt. Bring the pot to a boil and cook at a slow but steady boil for 1/2 hour.

Remove the chili pepper and boil the meat one hour longer. Add the marjoram and thyme and all the vegetables except the peas. Add the remaining beef stock. Simmer for 1 1/2 hours longer, stirring occasionally.

Set the pot aside to cool, and then place it in the refrigerator. At 1 1/2 hours before serving time, skim any congealed fat from the top of the pot, and place the stew pot on the stove. Beginning with a medium-low light to prevent burning, gradually increase the heat and bring it to a boil. Stir frequently and scrape the bottom of the pot to prevent the stew from burning. When the stew begins to bubble, reduce the heat to low until ready to serve. Prepare the peas according to the package directions and stir them into the stew just before serving.

Serves four.

Hearty Beef and Vegetable Kettle

> 2 pounds boneless chuck steak (not chuck roast)
> 1/2 cup all-purpose flour
> 1 teaspoon salt
> 1/2 teaspoon black pepper
> 1/2 teaspoon paprika
> 2 tablespoons olive oil
> 1 cup diced onion
> 6 cups water
> 1 1/2 teaspoon fines herbs
> 3 cups canned fire-roasted tomatoes, drained
> 2 cups carrots cut into 1-inch pieces
> 1 cup celery cut into 1/2-inch pieces
> 3 cups russet potatoes, peeled, cut in half lengthwise and then cut into 1-inch pieces
> 3 tablespoons cornstarch, blended with cold water to make a thin paste
> 1 cup frozen green peas

Trim most of the fat from the beef. Cut the beef into 1-inch cubes. Mix together the flour, salt, pepper and paprika. Dredge the beef in the flour mixture and shake off any excess flour. Heat the oil over medium high heat in a Dutch oven until very hot. Brown the beef in the oil on all sides. Set the beef aside.

Add the onions to the Dutch oven and brown lightly. (Add more oil if needed.) Return the beef to the Dutch oven. Add the water and fines herbs. Simmer, covered, for 30 minutes. Add the tomatoes, carrots, celery and potatoes. Simmer covered for 30 more minutes. Let the kettle cool and then put it in the refrigerator for several hours. Take the kettle out of the refrigerator and skim the fat.

Bring the kettle to a boil. Lower the heat to a slow boil. Stir in the cornstarch paste and stir until thick. Add green peas and cook till they are done.

Serve with crusty French bread and small green salad.

Serves eight.

Short Ribs

> 4 pounds short ribs
> 2 tablespoons olive oil (not extra virgin)
> 3/4 teaspoon salt
> 1/4 teaspoon ground black pepper
> 1 bay leaf
> 1 small onion, chopped
> 2 ribs of celery, chopped
> 1/4 teaspoon each of marjoram and thyme
> 1/2 cup dry red wine
> 1 cup of salt-free, fat-skimmed beef stock
> 8 ounces no-salt-added tomato sauce
> 1 tablespoon butter
> 1 tablespoon flour

Select meaty short ribs with as little fat as possible, and trim any large pieces of fat from the ribs. Don't buy flanken ribs because there is not enough meat on them. (Some places sell short ribs as cross-cut ribs.) Wash the ribs to rub off any splinters of bone. Pat them dry.

Heat the oil in a heavy Dutch oven. Brown the ribs thoroughly in batches in the oil. Pour off fat as it accumulates. Add the salt, pepper, bay leaf, onion, celery, marjoram, thyme, wine, beef stock and tomato sauce to the pot. Bring the mixture to a boil and simmer, covered, until the meat is fork-tender, about 1 hour.

Remove the short ribs to a plate and cover tightly with tinfoil to keep them warm. Melt the butter in a pan, add the flour, and whisk it into the butter until the flour is browned to make a roux. Stir the roux into the pan juices. Bring the sauce to a slow boil, stirring occasionally. Strain the gravy and serve it over the ribs.

I serve this with mashed potatoes.

Makes four servings.

Western Bean Pot

> 2 pounds of dried pinto beans
> water
> 1 teaspoon salt
> 2 large brown onions, diced
> 4 garlic cloves, minced
> 1 can (7 ounces) chopped green chilies (mild or hot, to taste)
> 1 can (28 ounces) tomatoes, preferably fire roasted
> 1 cup prepared tomato salsa (medium or hot, to taste)
> 1 teaspoon ground cumin
> 1/2 teaspoon red chili powder (optional, to taste)
> 1 cup diced smoked ham (optional)

Rinse the beans. Put the beans in a pot and add cold water to 2 inches above top of the beans. Soak the beans at least six hours. Drain and wash the beans and place them in a deep saucepan. Fill the pan with fresh water to about 2 inches above beans. Add the salt, cover and cook at a slow boil about 1 hour. Add water if needed.

Add all the other ingredients (except the ham), and stir into the beans. Make sure there is enough water to cover the beans by about 1 inch. Simmer 1 1/2 hours longer. Remove the pan from the heat, and stir in the ham. Cover and let sit to warm the ham, about 15 minutes.

Serve with heated flour tortillas for a hearty main dish on cold winter evenings or as a side dish with barbeque.

Makes a large amount of beans, enough for a group or to freeze portions for later use.

The Essential Stocks

With the investment of a little time and effort, you can improve the quality of what you are cooking at home by loading your freezer with an assortment of homemade stocks. Not only are they the foundation of many dishes, they also are essential for really good, quick work-day meals.

Many of the recipes in this book call for stock. In my kitchen it's always homemade. The first key to a great stock is to roast the bones before using them. (This should not be done with fish bones.) Traditionalists will cook the stock slowly for 24 hours and reduce the liquid to make a concentrate. I don't go that far. A slow boil for two or three hours will produce a perfectly good stock. It's a good idea to let the stock cool in the refrigerator and skim the fat before using it or freezing it for future use.

Beef Stock or Lamb Stock

For beef stock: Use 3 pounds beef soup bones (neck bones, marrow bones, or beef knuckle).

For lamb stock: Use the bone from a leg of lamb you have roasted, or buy a couple of lamb shanks and roast them before using for the stock.

- 3 quarts water
- 2 laurel bay leaves
- 1 large carrot, scrubbed and sliced
- 2 celery stalks, cut into 2-inch pieces, with leaves
- 2 medium onions, quartered
- 1 teaspoon coarse salt

Roast the bones in a 350-degree oven for 45 minutes. Put the bones into a soup pot along with the rest of the ingredients. Bring to a boil. Cook at a slow boil, covered, for 2 to 3 hours. Remove and discard the bones, vegetables and bay leaves. Strain the stock to remove any bone fragments. Put the stock in the refrigerator for 24 hours. Skim the fat. Freeze in 1 and 2-cup portions.

Turkey or Chicken Stock

> leftover bones from a roasted turkey and/or chicken
> 2 large carrots, scrubbed and sliced
> 2 celery stalks, cut into 2-inch pieces (leaves included; add extra leaves if you have them)
> 2 large onions, cut into eighths
> 1 parsnip, scrubbed and sliced
> 3 laurel bay leaves
> 1 teaspoon coarse salt
> 1 teaspoon whole black peppers
> 3 1/2 quarts water or more, to cover the bones and vegetables

Place a generous amount of roasted bones in a large stockpot. Add the carrots, celery, onion, parsnip, bay leaves, salt, pepper and water. Bring to a boil, reduce the heat and cook at a slow boil about 2 hours.

Remove and discard the bones and bay leaves. Strain stock to remove the vegetables. Put the stock in the refrigerator for 24 hours. Skim the fat. Freeze in 1 and 2-cup portions.

Important note: Do not use the carcass of a turkey that has been stuffed. Also, you cannot use parts of a turkey or chicken that has been flavored with herbs or spices or marinated, as that will give an unwanted taste to the stock. If you don't have the necessary turkey or chicken parts, buy them, roast them, and then use them to make a stock.

Fish Stock

> 2 pounds fish bones and/or heads
> 1 onion, cut into quarters
> 2 celery stalks, cut into 2-inch pieces, with leaves
> 2 carrots, scrubbed and cut into pieces
> water to cover

Put all the ingredients into a saucepan. Bring to a boil over medium heat. Reduce the heat to a simmer. Skim the foam that forms on the top. Simmer 1 hour.

Strain the stock through a fine strainer. Let it cool and then freeze it in 1 and 2-cup portions.

Vegetable Stock

> 2 large onions
> 1 pound carrots, peeled
> 2 pounds leeks, white part only
> 1 large turnip, peeled
> 3 tablespoons olive oil
> 1 bunch of parsley
> 3 bay leaves
> 4 quarts of water

Dice the onions, carrots, leeks and turnip. Heat the olive oil in a 250-degree oven in a glass or ceramic roasting pan. Add the diced vegetables and coat with the olive oil. Roast the vegetables for 30 minutes.

Put the vegetables into a stock pot. Add the parsley, bay leaves and water. Bring to a boil and reduce the heat to simmer for 30 minutes.

Remove the bay leaves and parsley. Put the vegetables and some of the broth in a blender and puree. Strain the broth through a very fine strainer. Use a double layer of cheesecloth if you don't have a very fine strainer. Add the strained broth to the rest of the broth. Let it cool for 30 minutes. Freeze in 1-cup portions.

TIPS FOR USING THESE RECIPES

The recipes in this book are guidelines. As written, they can lead you to wonderful meals, but they are not carved in stone. Every one of these recipes has evolved over time and continues to evolve today in my kitchen and the homes of my two sons. I hope you will add your own touches as you become familiar with them.

Please don't be shy about substituting ingredients to your personal tastes. If there is something that just isn't in your pantry when you decide to cook from one of these recipes, trust your imagination. Generations before you have done just that.

My son Lloyd recently was getting ready to cook a brisket for a dinner party. He discovered he didn't have a roasting pan large enough for the brisket he had purchased. So he cut the brisket in half and got out his slow cooker. Then he decided to substitute beer for the red wine called for in the recipe. The result, he said, was just as good. The recipe had gone through its latest evolution. What began as Aunt Tillie's recipe had become mine, and now was Lloyd's.

For decades I served chicken fricassee for dinner. One night I went to my pantry for a can of diced tomatoes. I found the only ones I had were fire-roasted, so I used those. It transformed the dish into something spectacular, so good that I substitute fire-roasted tomatoes in other recipes that call for canned tomatoes. It's the only way I would think of preparing chicken fricassee now—until the time comes when I go to the pantry and find I forgot to replenish my supply of fire-roasted tomatoes and I'm forced to improvise again.

Even the oldest of these recipes, the ones handed down through the generations in my family, are not sacrosanct. I've made adjustments to recipes handed down by my mother, who got them from her mother. And since neither of them ever used a written recipe, you can imagine how things have changed through the years.

I seldom cook the same thing the same way twice. There's no predicting which container of herbs I'll pull from the shelf for an omelet. Dried porcini mushrooms were the staple for my chicken in mushroom sauce until I decided to substitute dried morels one night. I braised pot roast with potatoes for years before I decided to add carrots to the braising pan.

So, feel free to treat the recipes in this book as a roadmap and supply your own side trips. Don't feel obligated to prepare anything precisely to the recipe, even the first time you cook it. Or, go ahead and follow the recipe the first time and decide what you will change the next time. It's one of the joys of being a home cook. No cookbook, including this one, should be devoid of your notes and scribbling in the margins.

- Use dried herbs rather than fresh whenever herbs are called for unless specified as fresh.
- Whenever you use dried herbs, put them in the palm of your hand and crush them with the thumb of the other hand before adding them to what you are cooking. It releases the flavor of the oils.
- When roasting or broiling on a rack in the oven, line the roasting pan with tinfoil first so the drippings don't burn and mar the pan. It makes it easier to clean the pan after.

- Assume any recipe that calls for olive oil means extra-virgin olive oil, unless otherwise designated.
- Extra-virgin olive oil will burn at a lower heat than other oils. If you are cooking something that needs high heat, think about using plain olive oil, or some other vegetable oil.
- When preparing to sauté, first put the pan on the stove over a medium-low heat. When the pan is nice and warm, add the oil. It should ripple but not smoke.
- The chicken recipes in this book call for the use of thighs or legs and thighs. That's because I find those to be the most flavorful parts of the chicken, and my cardiologist says the difference between these parts and the supposedly more healthful (lower-fat) breasts is negligible. If you prefer the breast, go ahead and make the substitution. But remember, the breast will cook more quickly than the dark meat and will dry out if overcooked.
- I'm sure you will have read or heard somewhere that mushrooms should not be washed. My favorite chef, Jacques Pepin, says to go ahead and wash them in cold water, but do it just as you are ready to use them. Jennifer hates finding grit in her food, so I wash my mushrooms under cold water and then dry them on a towel.
- Whenever you are making a stock or broth to freeze for later use, let it set in the refrigerator for 24 hours and then skim off the congealed fat before portioning the broth into one or two-cup freezer containers.
- For all recipes in this book that call for stocks or broth assume you will be using homemade stocks or broths. It's part of our effort to control the salt content in the recipe.
- I find recipes in most cookbooks call for more salt than necessary. So, I tend to cook with little or no salt and

add the salt to the final product as needed to enhance the flavor. My cardiologist loves me for this. For the recipes in this book, follow the directions and then add salt later, if needed, after tasting what you have produced.
- I use granulated garlic and onion throughout instead of garlic powder or onion powder because I find it blends more evenly into the cooking process and doesn't clump.
- For any recipe that calls for butter, use unsalted butter.

INDEX OF RECIPES

A

APPETIZERS
   Ceviche 269
   Chopped Liver (á la Tillie Tooter) 203
   Gravlaks a la Scandia 152
   Guacamole 81
   Potato Latkes Dad's Way 25
   Romanian Eggplant Salad 22
   Rumaki Spread 111
   Sui Mai 113
   Swedish Meatballs, Scandia Style Appetizers 149

B

BARBECUE
   Larry's Original Barbecue Sauce 91
   Ribs, Spare/Baby Back/St. Louis 90
   Stovetop Barbecue Chicken 92
Basque Chicken 126
BEANS
   Barbecue Style 93
   Chicken with Black Beans and Rice 189
   Southwest Black Beans and Chicken 94
   Western Bean Pot 295

BEEF
   Beef Burgundy 288
   Beef Stew 289
   Beef Stroganoff Marsala 230
   Beef Tacos 72
   Beef with Noodles and Cheese 30
   Brisket of Beef, Larry's Baked 205
   Hearty Beef and Vegetable Kettle 291
   Meat Loaf, Jennifer's Best in the World 162
   Pot Roast with Vegetables 183
   Short Ribs 293
   Steak Ranchero 79
   Swedish Meatballs, Scandia Style Appetizer 149
BREAKFAST
   About Omelets 134
   Breakfast Potatoes 139
   Chicken Livers and Eggs 231
   Eggs Creole 138
   Leftover Pork Roast Hash 140
   LEO (Lox, Eggs, and Onions) 137
BROOKLYN TRADITIONAL
   Kosher Dill Pickles 61
   Pushcart Charlotte Russe 60

Soda Fountain Black-and-White 48
Soda Fountain Egg Cream 50

C

Cheese Enchiladas 75
CHICKEN
    Barbecue, Stovetop 92
    Basque 126
    Cacciatore 273
    Chop Suey 115
    Chow Mein 116
    Curried 177
    Enchiladas 77
    Fricassee 274
    Gumbo Soup 270
    Herb-Baked 278
    In Mushroom Sauce 190
    Lemon 279
    Oven and Wedge Fries 280
    Pita Pockets with Cucumber-Tomato Relish 271
    Pot Pie 276
    Roast, Chinese Style 108
    Soup, Norma Levine's 12
    Tacos 74
    Tandoori 281
    With Black Beans and Rice 189
    With Southwest Black Beans 94
CHICKEN LIVER
    Chopped Liver Appetizer (á la Tillie Tooter) 203
    Livers and Eggs 231
    Rumaki Spread 111
    Tillie's Chicken Livers with Mushrooms, Onions and Sweetbreads 204
CHINESE
    Chop Suey, Chicken 115
    Chop Suey, Shrimp 115
    Chow Mein, Chicken 116
    Fried Rice 112
    Inspiration Shrimp 117
    Roast Chicken 108
    Roast Pork Two Ways 109
    Rumaki Spread 111
    Sui Mai 113
Cioppino 267

D

DESSERTS
    Apple Pie, Latticed 251
    Biscuit Tortoni 250
    Cheesecake 249
    Pushcart Charlotte Russe 60
    Strawberry Glaze Pie 252

E

EGGS
    About Omelets 134
    Chicken Livers and Eggs 231
    Eggs Creole 138
    LEO (Lox, Eggs, and Onions) 137
ENCHILADAS
    Cheese Enchiladas 75
    Chicken Enchiladas 77

F

FISH/SEAFOOD
    Ceviche 269
    Cioppino 267
    Gefilte Fish, Norma Levine's (hand written version) 32

Gefilte Fish, Norma Levine's (user-friendly translation) 34
Grandpa Larry's Poached Salmon 218
Gravlaks a la Scandia 152
Horseradish for Gefilte Fish 36
Pickled Lox 24
Scampi 166
Seafood Filé Gumbo 185
Shrimp Chop Suey 115
Shrimp Curry 181
Shrimp, Inspiration 117
Shrimp, Linguine with 165
Shrimp Marsala 163
Shrimp Ranchero 80

FRENCH
Beef Burgundy 288
Chicken Fricassee 274
Leg of Lamb 168

G

GREEK
Lemon Chicken 279
Moussaka 239

GUMBO
Chicken Gumbo Soup 270
Seafood Filé Gumbo 185
Turkey, Leftover Gumbo 286

I

INDIAN
Curried Chicken 177
Lamb Curry 179
Leg of Lamb 168
Shrimp Curry 181
Tandoori Chicken 281

ITALIAN
Biscuit Tortoni 250
Chicken Cacciatore 273
Cioppino 267
Leg of Lamb 168

J

JEWISH
Beef, Barley, and Mushroom Soup, Old-Country 16
Beef, Larry's Baked Brisket of 205
Cabbage, Stuffed 28
Chicken Soup, Norma Levine's 12
Dill Pickles, Kosher 61
Gefilte Fish, Norma Levine's (hand written version) 32
Gefilte Fish, Norma Levine's (user-friendly translation) 34
Horseradish for Gefilte Fish 36
Lokshen Kugel (Noodle Pie) 27
Lox, Pickled 24
Matzo Balls (Knaidlach) 14
Potato Latkes Dad's Way 25

L

LAMB
Curry 179
Leg of Lamb
French style 168
Indian style 168
Italian style 168
Middle Eastern style 169
Moussaka 239

Shanks 171
Shepherd's Pie 175
Shoulder Chops 167
Stew, American 173
Stew, Irish 174

M

Matzo Balls (Knaidlach) 14
MEXICAN
  Chili con Carne 70
  Enchiladas, Cheese 75
  Enchiladas, Chicken 77
  Guacamole 81
  Rice, Spanish 82
  Shrimp Ranchero 80
  Steak Ranchero 79
  Tacos, Beef 72
  Tacos, Chicken 74
MIDDLE EASTERN
  Chicken Pita Pockets with Cucumber-Tomato Relish 271
  Eggplant Salad, Romanian 22
  Leg of Lamb 169
Moussaka 239

N

NOODLES
  Beef with Noodles and Cheese 30
  Lokshen Kugel (Noodle Pie) 27

O

Omelets, About 134

P

PASTA
  Grandma Jennifer's Baked Spaghetti with Garden Sauce 216
  Linguine with Shrimp 165
PORK
  Chops, Oh, Those Golden 192
  Leftover, Roast Hash 140
  Ribs, Barbecue 90
  Roast, Chinese 109

R

RICE
  Chinese Fried 112
  Spanish 82
ROMANIAN
  Eggplant Salad 22
RUSSIAN
  Beef Stroganoff Marsala 230
  Cabbage Soup, Sweet-and-Sour Russian 20
  Stuffed Cabbage 28

S

SALAD
  Eggplant Salad, Romaanian 22
SIDE DISHES
  Lokshen Kugel (Noodle Pie) 27
  Potato Latkes Dad's Way 25
SOUP
  Beef, Barley, and Mushroom, Old-Country 16

Cabbage, Sweet-and-Sour
    Russian 20
Chicken Gumbo 270
Chicken, Norma Levine's 12
Cioppino 267
Gazpacho Like Scandia
    Used to Make 150
Navy Bean 18
Turkey, Leftover 287

SPANISH
Basque Chicken 126
Gazpacho Like Scandia
    Used to Make 150
Spanish Rice 82
Think-Thin Paella 187

STEW
Beef Burgundy 288
Beef Stew 289
Hearty Beef and Vegetable
    Kettle 291
Lamb Stew, American 173
Lamb Stew, Irish 174

STOCKS
The Essential Stocks
    Beef or Lamb 296
    Fish 298
    Turkey or Chicken 297
    Vegetable 298

SWEDISH
Gravlaks a la Scandia 152
Meatballs Scandia Style
    Appetizer 149

T

TURKEY
Gumbo, Leftover 286
Roasted, with Dripping
    Gravy 282
Soup, Leftover 287

V

VEGETABLES
Potatoes, Breakfast 139
Potato Latkes Dad's Way 25

ACKNOWLEDGMENTS

Thank you to Jennifer, my wife, for your patient understanding of the important role so many other women have played in my life and continue to play today. We never can know what's in another person's head, even after fifty years together. But I think you know that among all the women who have populated my life, you stand alone. And thank you too for proofreading this manuscript.

Thank you to Tracey Poirier for proofreading this manuscript and for surviving the tedious task of proofing the recipes. As we discussed some of the chapters of this book from time to time, your thoughts and input helped enhance the final text.

If there are any surviving typos in this book, it isn't the fault of Jennifer, Tracey, or any of the friends, relatives and former high school classmates who volunteered to proof read a chapter or two. I learned many years ago as a newspaper reporter, that typos are insidious critters; they hide, sometimes in plain sight, and then pop up later in strange places. In this era of electronic publishing, we can (and will) go back and squash them as they show their nasty little heads.

Thank you to Larry Dietz, an editor whose personality changes when he's editing. Mild-mannered and jocular Larry becomes a dictator. He refuses to allow me to begin a sentence with "and" or "but" or "so". So, if you miss those in my breezy writing style, blame the other Larry. His contributions as an editor greatly improved this work.

In a never-ending, fanatical drive to attempt to ferret out every typographical error, I invited assorted groups of friends, relatives and acquaintances to volunteer to help with the proof reading. For proofing one or more chapters, thank you to Evelyn Alexander, Kim Bossley, Shari Boyd, Carole Bregman, Gene Bregman, Frances Carey, Tim Carey, Irv Cherno, Mike Cornner, Jeff Daar, Marti Devore, Nancy Dolan, Mary Ellen Early, Mollie Early, Harvey Englander, Karen Fishwick, Victor Griego, Lisa Hansen, Rebecca Hoggarth, Shelly Levine (no relation), Linda Mann, Paula Morgan, Amy Nordahl, Jeff Resnick, Larry Sheingold, Parke Skelton, Linda Stone, Jean Vogel, Sylvia Witz, and Rod Wright.

To Fred Palmarino and Kevin Bush at Lancer Media, thank you for your creativity and support in so many ways.

Alison Holen at Archway Publishing, you stopped me in my tracks with your outstanding design of the book cover. Jenn Handy, at Archway, the hours you spent on the design of the complex interior of the book is apparent on every page. And Tim Fitch, my Archway concierge, thank you for your assistance.

Thank you to all the women who have been so important to my personal and professional life. You have challenged me, built me up, softened me, and allowed me to reveal myself to you. Not all of you have made it into this book, but all of you have a place in my warmest thoughts.

Posthumous thanks go to Kathy Hubert, who worked with me and for me for twenty-four years. She was there with me at the food court in the Fashion Square Mall when I first got the idea for this book.

A posthumous thank-you as well to my mother, Norma Levine, who cheered me on as I went on dates in high school that were not like those of the other guys. She called them "cosmopolitan," which defined her younger life and became infused in me. And thanks to my father, who set the prime example of a commitment to justice and equality.

CPSIA information can be obtained
at www.ICGtesting.com
Printed in the USA
LVHW040752170520
655736LV00003B/112